# This Refluent Stream

Layout has been optimised for comfort...

**To order additional copies of this book, contact:**
Xlibris
UK TFN: 0800 0148620 (Toll Free inside the UK)
UK Local: (02) 0369 56328 (+44 20 3695 6328 from outside the UK)
www.Xlibrispublishing.co.uk
Orders@Xlibrispublishing.co.uk
799927

# This Refluent Stream

## By

## M. E. Jones

# FOREWORD

The poems contained in this book were composed between 2002 and 2022.  I have arranged the poems so that when read in the order in which they have been presented, it will hopefully flow as a story or journey.  There might be some words or terms in the poems that readers may be unfamiliar with, so I have tried to include these in the glossary for quick reference.

Thanks for choosing to read this book, I hope you enjoy it.

M. E. Jones.
May 2022.

# Contents

## A Self Portrait

A lonely gate
In its entirety
The wood dense
The bolts sure
It locks shut;
It opens up.
A lonely gate
Supports each shadow
Each wren that rests
Upon such slumber
Solitude its bride;
In apogee they reside.
A lonely gate
Stands alone
If ever there was a fence
The fence has gone
A wooden heart
With nothing to hold
Closed within its own frame;
Open only to the cold.

Until the winter drifts
Had gathered all around
A lonely gate;
And the path it found...

# A Self Portrait

A lonely gate
In its entirety
The wood dense
The bolts sure
It locks shut;
It opens up.
A lonely gate
Supports each shadow
Each wren that rests
Upon such slumber
Solitude its bride;
In apogee they reside.
A lonely gate
Stands alone
If ever there was a fence
The fence has gone
A wooden heart
With nothing to hold
Closed within its own frame;
Open only to the cold.

Until the winter drifts
Had gathered all around
A lonely gate;
And the path it found...

## Sun in Setting
### (a tree looking into a puddle)

My reflection ripples as the sky opens up
I needed that window to sprawl upon
Love once held my hand as if it were a sill
And carved initials of a time overdue
For if you forever leave the curtains drawn
There will be no autumnal hues
*No reds, no golds, no sunsets, no moon*
So please give my tears a chance to fall
Into the depths of that reflection
To find love buds my branches next spring
Then I will cover this puddle
With such a nurturing dappling shadow
Resting upon that sun now setting
As the weary lean against a lamppost
And the nadir removes all exceptions
So if you glance out of your window
And you happen to notice this tree
Collapsing down into its own reflection
Mirrored as I am and will always be
In reds and golds revealing sunset
Holding the moon aloft for you to see
Perhaps then you might ajar your window
Upon which I was tapping impatiently
Then please accept this acorn
And find somewhere to bury it deep
Because all I have here is this puddle
Upon this lonely island of concrete

## Sun in Setting
### (a tree looking into a puddle)

My reflection ripples as the sky opens up
I needed that window to sprawl upon
Love once held my hand as if it were a sill
And carved initials of a time overdue
For if you forever leave the curtains drawn
There will be no autumnal hues
*No reds, no golds, no sunsets, no moon*
So please give my tears a chance to fall
Into the depths of that reflection
To find love buds my branches next spring
Then I will cover this puddle
With such a nurturing dappling shadow
Resting upon that sun now setting
As the weary lean against a lamppost
And the nadir removes all exceptions
So if you glance out of your window
And you happen to notice this tree
Collapsing down into its own reflection
Mirrored as I am and will always be
In reds and golds revealing sunset
Holding the moon aloft for you to see
Perhaps then you might ajar your window
Upon which I was tapping impatiently
Then please accept this acorn
And find somewhere to bury it deep
Because all I have here is this puddle
Upon this lonely island of concrete

## Petals

I held a buttercup under your chin,
Your skin was so golden glow.
Too few the daisies so short the chain,
I kept one with me, I pluck it now...
She loves me,
She loves me not,
She loves me,
She loves me not,
Each petal falling to the ground,
Tear, after tear drop;
Until the setting sun was naked,
And the sun rose upon it's petals,
Love of the sun in golden glow...
A tear drop sunrise,
A tear drop sunset
I held a buttercup,
To catch the petals,,,,

## Homesick

The blue room
Train room
There once was a train
And a track
Sheet upon sheet
Upon that bed
A cross stich woollen blanket
Of reds and yellows
And green
The room was cold and blue
I've never felt warmer
I never will.

*three*

## Petals

I held a buttercup under your chin,
Your skin was so golden glow.
Too few the daisies so short the chain,
I kept one with me, I pluck it now...
She loves me,
She loves me not,
She loves me,
She loves me not,
Each petal falling to the ground,
Tear, after tear drop;
Until the setting sun was naked,
And the sun rose upon it's petals,
Love of the sun in golden glow...
A tear drop sunrise,
A tear drop sunset
I held a buttercup,
To catch the petals,,,,

## Homesick

The blue room
Train room
There once was a train
And a track
Sheet upon sheet
Upon that bed
A cross stich woollen blanket
Of reds and yellows
And green
The room was cold and blue
I've never felt warmer
I never will.

*three*

## A Place for Everything and....

How prim and proper that border,
Bordering a finely cut lawn.
The annuals like furniture,
Perennials a merry mess or clutter.
But no leek in flower,
No cabbage for a butterfly,
No lettuce there long enough
To put on a flowering show.
Seeds come in packets,
Vegetables displayed at markets,
The warning was understood.
The right place for everything,
Is freedom to love and grow.
A compost heap, a woodpile rotting,
A railway bridge across a river;
Another across a badger den,
Spanning a field of rabbit burrows,
What a treasure if up pops a mole!
You have dominium to- not of the animals,
Do not trample this Earth gazing ever upwards,
The Moon holds on to the earth in gravitas,
As there is but one to hold.

So, hold tight the Earth,

Or let it go.

# A Place for Everything and....

How prim and proper that border,
Bordering a finely cut lawn.
The annuals like furniture,
Perennials a merry mess or clutter.
But no leek in flower,
No cabbage for a butterfly,
No lettuce there long enough
To put on a flowering show.
Seeds come in packets,
Vegetables displayed at markets,
The warning was understood.
The right place for everything,
Is freedom to love and grow.
A compost heap, a woodpile rotting,
A railway bridge across a river;
Another across a badger den,
Spanning a field of rabbit burrows,
What a treasure if up pops a mole!
You have dominium to- not of the animals,
Do not trample this Earth gazing ever upwards,
The Moon holds on to the earth in gravitas,
As there is but one to hold.

So, hold tight the Earth,

Or let it go.

## Fossilised Remanences

I walked the nautical mile
Now I sit...
Those mountains with fangs biting up
Will just have to go around me
I'm on a life strike.
There is no harmony,
To check mate one's self;
What a victory!
I threw that Frisbee,
It lies now on the ground...
I was thrown the nautical mile.
Now I sit...
Littering this land
Gift me a disc to shine upon me,
That place where the field is visible!
And then reflected in the Moon.
Why wait?
This river made rock smooth pebble,
I am jagged with teeth biting up.
I walked the nautical mile
Now I sit...
With that dancing mirror above,
Corral clothing my hull,
I'm emotionally wrecked;
The only treasure I carried was love.
Is it all now dead?


It appears the sail is set...
They never broke this anchor,
Now I remain...
To walk the nautical mile again.

## Fossilised Remanences

I walked the nautical mile
Now I sit...
Those mountains with fangs biting up
Will just have to go around me
I'm on a life strike.
There is no harmony,
To check mate one's self;
What a victory!
I threw that Frisbee,
It lies now on the ground...
I was thrown the nautical mile.
Now I sit...
Littering this land
Gift me a disc to shine upon me,
That place where the field is visible!
And then reflected in the Moon.
Why wait?
This river made rock smooth pebble,
I am jagged with teeth biting up.
I walked the nautical mile
Now I sit...
With that dancing mirror above,
Corral clothing my hull,
I'm emotionally wrecked;
The only treasure I carried was love.
Is it all now dead?


It appears the sail is set...
They never broke this anchor,
Now I remain...
To walk the nautical mile again.

## Skeleton Key

I have a key ring
Yet have no key
Just a souvenir
Kept in my pocket
Sometimes it is washed
Within the pocket of the pants
Regardless of how clean
Hung upon a holder
I can open no locks
Not a single conversation
Or reminiscence
I would not be picked
For anything
But I have my past
And if I think back far enough
I might just out last
Myself to when I was free
To choose a path
Now the path chooses me
Find my hand upon clocks
Seeming so stationary
But don't extrapolate
Lonely is yet lonely
I keep this skeleton within me
We could never get out

I had no key
I had no key
I had no key
I had no key
I had no key
I had no key
I had no key
I had no key
I had no key
I had no key
I had no key
I had no key
I had no key
I had no key
I had no key
I had no key
I had no key

## Skeleton Key

I have a key ring
Yet have no key
Just a souvenir
Kept in my pocket
Sometimes it is washed
Within the pocket of the pants
Regardless of how clean
Hung upon a holder
I can open no locks
Not a single conversation
Or reminiscence
I would not be picked
For anything
But I have my past
And if I think back far enough
I might just out last
Myself to when I was free
To choose a path
Now the path chooses me
Find my hand upon clocks
Seeming so stationary
But don't extrapolate
Lonely is yet lonely
I keep this skeleton within me
We could never get out

I had no key
I had no key
I had no key
I had no key
I had no key
I had no key
I had no key
I had no key
I had no key
I had no key
I had no key
I had no key
I had no key
I had no key
I had no key
I had no key

# Saved

So many dreams profound
Don't dismiss them all
I was there or will be
It is the future of all or none
Do you want this sweet
Or make this bitter me
I had a tear, I saved it
I was, am and will be.

# Seeds

The seed landed
Sapling sprouted
Up and counting
Left there hanging
The capo fretting
Where tears are pooling
And this fool

Plucking the right string
On the wrong side of the bridge

The seed landed
Sapling sprouted
A capo clamping neck
Left there hanging
And this fool

Wasting every breath...

# Saved

So many dreams profound
Don't dismiss them all
I was there or will be
It is the future of all or none
Do you want this sweet
Or make this bitter me
I had a tear, I saved it
I was, am and will be.

# Seeds

The seed landed
Sapling sprouted
Up and counting
Left there hanging
The capo fretting
Where tears are pooling
And this fool

Plucking the right string
On the wrong side of the bridge

The seed landed
Sapling sprouted
A capo clamping neck
Left there hanging
And this fool

Wasting every breath...

# Candela (love at first sight)

When she blew out the candle
It drew breath of darkness
Then gasped once urgently
The field returned in flame
She did not fall but instead paused
In awe of the candle that lit itself

She could see her plates stacked up
On the shelf as they always were
All immaculate except for the plate on top
The only plate ever used then cleaned
Cups the same as new but for one
Polished from care in cradling

She went out in search of a companion
And love drew in a breath
So quick was she to find a lock
Yet so slow to craft the key
And some locks open with a kiss

When she blew out the candle

I drew breath of darkness
Then gasped once urgently
The field returned in flame
She did not fall but instead paused
In awe of the candle that lit itself

Yet again...

# Candela (love at first sight)

When she blew out the candle
It drew breath of darkness
Then gasped once urgently
The field returned in flame
She did not fall but instead paused
In awe of the candle that lit itself

She could see her plates stacked up
On the shelf as they always were
All immaculate except for the plate on top
The only plate ever used then cleaned
Cups the same as new but for one
Polished from care in cradling

She went out in search of a companion
And love drew in a breath
So quick was she to find a lock
Yet so slow to craft the key
And some locks open with a kiss

When she blew out the candle

I drew breath of darkness
Then gasped once urgently
The field returned in flame
She did not fall but instead paused
In awe of the candle that lit itself

Yet again...

# That Way

If we could move like that
Live out this music video
You could sing to my guitar
And I would lose myself in your tone.
Perhaps by the equinox
We could dance in moon light
If you have a field I can rake
A storm to keep you safe from.
Or maybe they just follow me
I had been a trouble maker
Now a do no more wronger
Lightening lights the way
As I dance trying to avoid it
I get by on patience
And day dreams
Big ideas that don't fit with theirs;
A long coat to keep out the rain
The longer the coat
The larger the bridge made
Across any puddle you might cross...
They might not see it that way
But then, who does?

## That Way

If we could move like that
Live out this music video
You could sing to my guitar
And I would lose myself in your tone.
Perhaps by the equinox
We could dance in moon light
If you have a field I can rake
A storm to keep you safe from.
Or maybe they just follow me
I had been a trouble maker
Now a do no more wronger
Lightening lights the way
As I dance trying to avoid it
I get by on patience
And day dreams
Big ideas that don't fit with theirs;
A long coat to keep out the rain
The longer the coat
The larger the bridge made
Across any puddle you might cross...
They might not see it that way
But then, who does?

## Bumblebee Fretting

On every fret you buzz

You seek to find every nectar

Point me to your forever

Then back to the buzz

Songs of being lonely forever

Of bumblebeeing

In one place or another

In solitude.

We drift from one place

Then get pushed into another

When we next return that same way

It has all been cut down

We try to find another yet

You removed the access

To protect your infants

From a possible future

With hornets and bee stings

Imposing on them a future

With no insects in it.

## Bumblebee Fretting

On every fret you buzz
You seek to find every nectar
Point me to your forever
Then back to the buzz
Songs of being lonely forever
Of bumblebeeing
In one place or another
In solitude.
We drift from one place
Then get pushed into another
When we next return that same way
It has all been cut down
We try to find another yet
You removed the access
To protect your infants
From a possible future
With hornets and bee stings
Imposing on them a future
With no insects in it.

## Pea wilder

Hours spent grazing
These bees on nectar
You want to design it
At least carefully craft it!
Beatles the rotten wood
Fly's the rotting carcass
Crickets the grassing shoots
Deep and moist the larvae
Building an eco-system
A tree breathes in the sky
Weeds fill the spaces
Between the grasses
And they flower in unison
They send their seeds
Upon the changing movements
Another housing development
Pouring concrete so deep.
Could they have a meadow
Space for a large pond
With wildlife tracks under new roads
Welcome the mosquitoes
Save a place for wasps
For mice, bats and hedgehogs
Moles, ticks, termites, ants and vowels
Damsel flies, dragon flies
Otters, salmon, crayfish, mollusc
The razor clams
And in each shower room
A mirror.

# Pea wilder

Hours spent grazing
These bees on nectar
You want to design it
At least carefully craft it!
Beatles the rotten wood
Fly's the rotting carcass
Crickets the grassing shoots
Deep and moist the larvae
Building an eco-system
A tree breathes in the sky
Weeds fill the spaces
Between the grasses
And they flower in unison
They send their seeds
Upon the changing movements
Another housing development
Pouring concrete so deep.
Could they have a meadow
Space for a large pond
With wildlife tracks under new roads
Welcome the mosquitoes
Save a place for wasps
For mice, bats and hedgehogs
Moles, ticks, termites, ants and vowels
Damsel flies, dragon flies
Otters, salmon, crayfish, mollusc
The razor clams
And in each shower room
A mirror.

# Weeds

It invites pollinators
To suckle on its suns
The blues, yellows, reds,
Artistic pallet runs
And forms a space capsule
Into the unknown
With no mission control
Crash landing then a gentle gust
Then another lift-off
Until it settles upon their lawn
And digs in deep into their earth
We carry our soil, this body
Brain stem root
They cling to the earth
With shooting fingers
Then push towards the skies above
Creating those flowers again
A planet to a sun
A shadow to sun dial
Moth to flame
Weed killer to snuff it out
That kills more than any flame:
Weeds move much like we do
Plants and flowers stay the same
When tended to by determination
Otherwise they are all the same
Just weeds:
As are we all....

# Weeds

It invites pollinators
To suckle on its suns
The blues, yellows, reds,
Artistic pallet runs
And forms a space capsule
Into the unknown
With no mission control
Crash landing then a gentle gust
Then another lift-off
Until it settles upon their lawn
And digs in deep into their earth
We carry our soil, this body
Brain stem root
They cling to the earth
With shooting fingers
Then push towards the skies above
Creating those flowers again
A planet to a sun
A shadow to sun dial
Moth to flame
Weed killer to snuff it out
That kills more than any flame:
Weeds move much like we do
Plants and flowers stay the same
When tended to by determination
Otherwise they are all the same
Just weeds:
As are we all....

## With a Telescope

You turned my gaze
Balanced me pivot
Hold off the clouds
Set me up
Azimuth centred
Polaris centred
Now just turn
The Jupiterian moons
Skirt of Saturn
My eyes were opened up
They will never close.


## *I Made My Bed*

*I made my bed*
*I'll lye in it*
*Pour salt on the wound*
*For every scale*
*A measure and*
*For every verb a word.*
*Wash the sheet music*
*Hang it up*
*Upon that linen line,*
*I waited so long for*
*The hand to fall*
*So we could begin anew,*
*Now I dance to silence*
*In every darkened room*
*I sleep alone*
*I pour salt on the wound*
*As I dream of you*

## With a Telescope

You turned my gaze
Balanced me pivot
Hold off the clouds
Set me up
Azimuth centred
Polaris centred
Now just turn
The Jupiterian moons
Skirt of Saturn
My eyes were opened up
They will never close.

## *I Made My Bed*

*I made my bed*
*I'll lye in it*
*Pour salt on the wound*
*For every scale*
*A measure and*
*For every verb a word.*
*Wash the sheet music*
*Hang it up*
*Upon that linen line,*
*I waited so long for*
*The hand to fall*
*So we could begin anew,*
*Now I dance to silence*
*In every darkened room*
*I sleep alone*
*I pour salt on the wound*
*As I dream of you*

# Why Not?

Music changes mood
This poetry too
I have not eaten food
I am on holiday
Dreams do that
The ones in waking
Truth is in faking
My hand is shaking
Drink does that
I am on holiday
That is that.
Well not quite

I have purpose
Ring the cloth
That cleansed this mess
I made so much
Seen now in the cup
Changing ways
Always does
I am forever
Given up
To be judged
Well not quite but,
I diluted every cup.

# Why Not?

Music changes mood
This poetry too
I have not eaten food
I am on holiday
Dreams do that
The ones in waking
Truth is in faking
My hand is shaking
Drink does that
I am on holiday
That is that.
Well not quite

I have purpose
Ring the cloth
That cleansed this mess
I made so much
Seen now in the cup
Changing ways
Always does
I am forever
Given up
To be judged
Well not quite but,
I diluted every cup.

## All Dressed Up With...

Why say the backing track
is a standard?
It responds to your breathing
In and out.
Clear note pure you sing,
Swelling dreamy piano.
Fill my soul, drain my doubt,
Let's forget my own music drought.
You and me as we always should be,
In love- together making beautiful music.
Let's just say you can see me different;
Differently from how I see myself.
Sad, lonely flower on a tree,
Weeping so long the bees settle,
Then the flower was gone.
My race to love was run.
All I have is these northern lights,
I know they are there, but I'll never see them.

## Shadow

*Facing the sun at dawn.*
*With each step,*
*...................I spill my shadow*

## All Dressed Up With...

Why say the backing track
is a standard?
It responds to your breathing
In and out.
Clear note pure you sing,
Swelling dreamy piano.
Fill my soul, drain my doubt,
Let's forget my own music drought.
You and me as we always should be,
In love- together making beautiful
music.
Let's just say you can see me different;
Differently from how I see myself.
Sad, lonely flower on a tree,
Weeping so long the bees settle,
Then the flower was gone.
My race to love was run.
All I have is these northern lights,
I know they are there, but I'll never
see them.


## Shadow

*Facing the sun at dawn.*
*With each step,*
*...................I spill my shadow*

## Road Block

The tallest tree
With its roots rooted deep
And you with a plan
And you with a crane
Crew, shovels, forks
Saws, axes, hammers
A big budget
The tallest tree
With no one to defend it
I block the progress of your road
As you block sense
The battle of young and old
But you remove the young as well
Plant new or stop
Before you can go no further
Idiots!

## Traffic Light

You had me at amber
At red I looked away
There might have been green
I was just in the way
What books on shelf
Will be read again
Which books will never be seen
What does a flashing amber mean?
Proceed with caution
From start to end.

## Road Block

The tallest tree
With its roots rooted deep
And you with a plan
And you with a crane
Crew, shovels, forks
Saws, axes, hammers
A big budget
The tallest tree
With no one to defend it
I block the progress of your road
As you block sense
The battle of young and old
But you remove the young as well
Plant new or stop
Before you can go no further
Idiots!

## Traffic Light

You had me at amber
At red I looked away
There might have been green
I was just in the way
What books on shelf
Will be read again
Which books will never be seen
What does a flashing amber mean?
Proceed with caution
From start to end.

## Feel the Strai

We spend like this our live
In moments we are tie
In between a rock and hard plac
Or in shelter from a storr
We quiver like this our live
Then place cups at each en
When all is calm we spea
That's when we look for friend
We need that tension in our live
Pull back to feel the strai
You feel it as you walk them to schoo
Wishing you could go back there agai
We spend like this our live
If we are lucky to the en
Then the fingers slip releasing that tensio
Sending an arrow to where it was aime

## Hour hand

The verb ran away,
That was expected,
But then verb waited,
Set, silent, stilled, with no hesitation;
Add another hour to the clock.

The dreams shadows play,
Death held at bay with the pill,
To stop the hidden clock,
Silent, stilled, set, with no awareness;
Another hour soon forgot.

**17:00**

## el the Strain

e spend like this our lives
moments we are tied
between a rock and hard place
· in shelter from a storm
e quiver like this our lives
ien place cups at each end
hen all is calm we speak
iat's when we look for friends
e need that tension in our lives
ill back to feel the strain
iu feel it as you walk them to school
ishing you could go back there again
e spend like this our lives
we are lucky to the end
ien the fingers slip releasing that tension
nding an arrow to where it was aimed

## Hour hand

The verb ran away,
That was expected,
But then verb waited,
Set, silent, stilled, with no hesitation;
Add another hour to the clock.

The dreams shadows play,
Death held at bay with the pill,
To stop the hidden clock,
Silent, stilled, set, with no awareness;
Another hour soon forgot.

**17:00**

## A life Long Test

I need a long life
To be successful
To learn how to spell write
And how to rhyme well
To add to the dust
To be part of the economy
That makes the furniture polish
To wipe myself away from me
I need a long life
To be a success
I finished ages ago
I'm bored, the examiner is bored too
Now we are both looking at the clock
Time is up, pens down;
We'll send you the results,
In a few months.

That's a long time sat at a desk.

## Rose Hips

The flower
Woody stems
Hooked thorns
Well known
The rose hip
Such a generous bounty
I've never eaten a single one

# A life Long Test

I need a long life
To be successful
To learn how to spell write
And how to rhyme well
To add to the dust
To be part of the economy
That makes the furniture polish
To wipe myself away from me
I need a long life
To be a success
I finished ages ago
I'm bored, the examiner is bored too
Now we are both looking at the clock
Time is up, pens down;
We'll send you the results,
In a few months.

That's a long time sat at a desk.

## Rose Hips

The flower
Woody stems
Hooked thorns
Well known
The rose hip
Such a generous bounty
I've never eaten a single one

## Nail Clippings

Thank you for this body I borrowed
I was born in it and shedding it as I go
I doubt it will last forever
But nothing ever made in forever has
Maybe next time I'll get a service
Treat my next body like my car
No- your car, mine is sat wondering where I am
Sorn off road, I walk while I can
I must remember to talk!
What was I saying?  Well typing...

Ah yes, the bit of us that is driving
Is being driven and driven and driven
And we can't all crash at once
So, look after your ever after
Treat yourself, to humiliating love.
When your nail clippings binned
And hair trimmings fly
Skin pledges to leave dust on the tv,
When it all falls away
What is left?

You, me, and everything else.

## Nail Clippings

Thank you for this body I borrowed
I was born in it and shedding it as I go
I doubt it will last forever
But nothing ever made in forever has
Maybe next time I'll get a service
Treat my next body like my car
No- your car, mine is sat wondering where I
am
Sorn off road, I walk while I can
I must remember to talk!
What was I saying? Well typing...

Ah yes, the bit of us that is driving
Is being driven and driven and driven
And we can't all crash at once
So, look after your ever after
Treat yourself, to humiliating love.
When your nail clippings binned
And hair trimmings fly
Skin pledges to leave dust on the tv,
When it all falls away
What is left?

You, me, and everything else.

## Casket

A body of work lies inside
Every case of cloven timber
In darkness we breathe free
There is no need to linger
Cast yourself out to into the field
Within which we are ever after
Better to rise into vivid dark
Than hear chain slip
Dropping anchor

Memories that go in want of rain
Or a venal pitter patter
Should not be stilled in frames so pin
As you hoist yourself from slumber
For if a pin should ring out loud
In such a space as none can hear
The rigging holds aloft the sail
Just as wooden ribs displace
Bodies of water

Ashes may fall down to earth
Dust rises upwards with the air
No final resting place found
Within that which is left to cinder
Choose moments you may want to relive
Satisfy your soulful hunger
Gift dreams to others such as you can inspire
Or warn of being you at your worst
Then retire.

**Twenty**

## Casket

A body of work lies inside
Every case of cloven timber
In darkness we breathe free
There is no need to linger
Cast yourself out to into the field
Within which we are ever after
Better to rise into vivid dark
Than hear chain slip
Dropping anchor

Memories that go in want of rain
Or a venal pitter patter
Should not be stilled in frames so pin
As you hoist yourself from slumber
For if a pin should ring out loud
In such a space as none can hear
The rigging holds aloft the sail
Just as wooden ribs displace
Bodies of water

Ashes may fall down to earth
Dust rises upwards with the air
No final resting place found
Within that which is left to cinder
Choose moments you may want to relive
Satisfy your soulful hunger
Gift dreams to others such as you can inspire
Or warn of being you at your worst
Then retire.

**Twenty**

## Carpet

I am that part near the door
You ask how I am as you enter
I am well (I am well worn)
You hear the answer
Assume the later
The only way to fix this
Rip the whole lot up
A patch will not suffice
For seeming might undo
A chance to lay across
The lay line
To hide under the bed
The wool pulled over
The rug pulled from under.

Can I remove myself
To be set down anew?
Can I reject myself
Then fear rejection no more?
Can I humiliate myself
Then fear humiliation no more?
Can I embrace myself
Then fear myself no more?
Practice makes perfect

Perfectly worn.

## Carpet

I am that part near the door
You ask how I am as you enter
I am well (I am well worn)
You hear the answer
Assume the later
The only way to fix this
Rip the whole lot up
A patch will not suffice
For seeming might undo
A chance to lay across
The lay line
To hide under the bed
The wool pulled over
The rug pulled from under.

Can I remove myself
To be set down anew?
Can I reject myself
Then fear rejection no more?
Can I humiliate myself
Then fear humiliation no more?
Can I embrace myself
Then fear myself no more?
Practice makes perfect

Perfectly worn.

# Binary

You make it seem so easy
Every inevitable romance
Which gets caught in lenses
And digital storage
Binary and hexadecimal
The numbers do not lie
So even the briefest encounter
Can last a life time
In your timeline

Like two candles
Side by side
Burning fiercely
Their melting wax mixing
As one becomes the other
And even if they are parted
They divide equally
And set in time
All they leave behind

I am a wick
I burn quickly
To where they put me
Birthday cake or TNT
Love is binary- on or off
Press that plunger
Strike a match
Scratch to spark
Love is a fire forever burning
Sharpest breath you steal the flame
I will always be returning

# Binary

You make it seem so easy
Every inevitable romance
Which gets caught in lenses
And digital storage
Binary and hexadecimal
The numbers do not lie
So even the briefest encounter
Can last a life time
In your timeline

Like two candles
Side by side
Burning fiercely
Their melting wax mixing
As one becomes the other
And even if they are parted
They divide equally
And set in time
All they leave behind

I am a wick
I burn quickly
To where they put me
Birthday cake or TNT
Love is binary- on or off
Press that plunger
Strike a match
Scratch to spark
Love is a fire forever burning
Sharpest breath you steal the flam
I will always be returning

## p pping bubble wrap

Life₀in₀a₀bubble₀wrap₀bubble₀
A₀dew₀drop₀dripping₀from₀a₀water₀spout₀₀
Can₀one₀wrap₀the₀other₀in₀maternal₀protection₀
and₀if₀so,₀for₀how₀long?₀

Perhaps₀until₀the₀joyful₀addictive₀pressure₀
Finds₀that₀final₀one₀to₀squeeze...₀

And₀then₀stops.

Until that dew droplet drops......................o
To₀form₀more₀bubbles₀cherished₀...o...o..o....o..o.o.....o
Squeezed₀tight₀until₀they₀p0p₀₀₀₀ o o o o

## Joints

A dove carrying a branch
In its beak
Can build itself a world
Like the one we have
That its tail holds together
So there is for a while
Somewhere, somehow;
Peace.

## p pping bubble wrap

Life。in。a。bubble。wrap。bubble。
A。dew。drop。dripping。from。a。water。spout。。
Can。one。wrap。the。other。in。maternal。protection。
and。if。so,。for。how。long?。

Perhaps。until。the。joyful。addictive。pressure。
Finds。that。final。one。to。squeeze…。

And。then。stops.

Until that dew droplet drops……………。
To。form。more。bubbles。cherished。…。…。。…。…。。。……。
Squeezed。tight。until。they。pOp。。。。  。  。      。  。

# Joints

A dove carrying a branch
In its beak
Can build itself a world
Like the one we have
That its tail holds together
So there is for a while
Somewhere, somehow;
Peace.

## The Absent Sadness

Have you seen my Sadness?
I lost it so long ago
It keeps grief in one pocket
What's in the other I don't know
Despair has begun to wonder
Whether Sadness is seeking solitude?
Greed is convinced Sorrow has found it
And is keeping it for itself
I can only blame myself
For withholding my gratitude

Have you felt my Sadness?
It might have passed you by
Perhaps your Joy was briefly dulled
Your Boldness becoming Shy
It wears a clock upon its wrist
But cares nothing of the time
Nostalgia recalls receiving that gift
But keeps that to itself
I can only blame myself
For refusing my need to cry.

Have you hidden my Sadness?
As my Scepticism suspects
Deep within the laughter lines
Wrapped in Shame and Regret
Grief is in one pocket
Upon its wrist is the time
I am feeling so lonely
But we keep that to our self
I can only blame myself
But we needed somewhere to hide.

## The Absent Sadness

Have you seen my Sadness?
I lost it so long ago
It keeps grief in one pocket
What's in the other I don't know
Despair has begun to wonder
Whether Sadness is seeking solitude?
Greed is convinced Sorrow has found it
And is keeping it for itself
I can only blame myself
For withholding my gratitude

Have you felt my Sadness?
It might have passed you by
Perhaps your Joy was briefly dulled
Your Boldness becoming Shy
It wears a clock upon its wrist
But cares nothing of the time
Nostalgia recalls receiving that gift
But keeps that to itself
I can only blame myself
For refusing my need to cry.

Have you hidden my Sadness?
As my Scepticism suspects
Deep within the laughter lines
Wrapped in Shame and Regret
Grief is in one pocket
Upon its wrist is the time
I am feeling so lonely
But we keep that to our self
I can only blame myself
But we needed somewhere to hide.

## Life Addiction

I don't enjoy this day to day
Depression you might call it
But I am not depressed
I am not feeling down, not yet
I just lack enough energy to get up
To get dressed
The TV taught me what happiness is
Maybe they are watching TV too
With no sound
Life itself never insisted on happiness
It never gave any guidelines
Life is an addiction
We keep seeking its end to begin again
Better to just die for good for the first time
Before we forget how to...

It seems life has many ways to keep us here
Pain that screams, pain that sorrows,
Pain that loves, pain that craves,
Pain that regrets, pain that regresses,
Pain that longs for acceptance
That longs for more kisses

I don't enjoy this addictive cycle
Of seeking life to fulfil
Screaming, sorrowful, loveless, craving, regretful, regressive,
longing,
abandon.

I'll finish this life, then I'm done with it....

## Life Addiction

I don't enjoy this day to day
Depression you might call it
But I am not depressed
I am not feeling down, not yet
I just lack enough energy to get up
To get dressed
The TV taught me what happiness is
Maybe they are watching TV too
With no sound
Life itself never insisted on happiness
It never gave any guidelines
Life is an addiction
We keep seeking its end to begin again
Better to just die for good for the first time
Before we forget how to...

It seems life has many ways to keep us here
Pain that screams, pain that sorrows,
Pain that loves, pain that craves,
Pain that regrets, pain that regresses,
Pain that longs for acceptance
That longs for more kisses

I don't enjoy this addictive cycle
Of seeking life to fulfil
Screaming, sorrowful, loveless, craving, regretful, regressive,
longing,
abandon.

I'll finish this life, then I'm done with it,

Yet ever to return.

## Ancestral

The shadow saw a light
It being but one alone
Was alone and was alone still.
The shadow saw another light
Realising no one can
Light the dark alone was still.. .
The shadow saw itself,
In the dark between the two;
Then shadows casting,
And wondered who is who?
As we always have,
And always do.. .. .. . . .. ... . ..


## Peacock

Birds of a feather,
Flags of their fathers,
Each their own banner,
Bringing them together,
Like minded?
Close knit?
For every grouping,
A loose stitch.
To say "this group is good",
"this group is bad",
Is to be cold in winter,
With arrow in back.

## Ancestral

The shadow saw a light
It being but one alone
Was alone and was alone still.
The shadow saw another light
Realising no one can
Light the dark alone was still.. .
The shadow saw itself,
In the dark between the two;
Then shadows casting,
And wondered who is who?
As we always have,
And always do.. .. .. . .. . ... . ..

## Peacock

Birds of a feather,
Flags of their fathers,
Each their own banner,
Bringing them together,
Like minded?
Close knit?
For every grouping,
A loose stitch.
To say "this group is good",
"this group is bad",
Is to be cold in winter,
With arrow in back.

## Two Readers (Wisdom then Youth)

*Deep down into this old chair*
I sit in an old chair
My old bones settle
*Deep down into this old chair*
Dock leaf and nettle
Cartlidge and muscle
*Deep down into this old chair*
This old chair creaks
Under the weight so
*Deep down into this old chair*
I rise to my feet
I cannot speak
*Deep down into this old chair*
I perch like a bird
Atop a sound I heard
*Deep down into this old chair*
No periodic table
Can define my use
*Deep down into this old chair*
No vacant office
Can find space to fill
*Deep down into this old chair*
This scaffold entwined
As day holds up the night
*Deep down into this old chair*
So old becomes new
For so many things grew
Deep down into this old chair

Younger readers may not need to rest regularly whilst reading this poem. Please feel
free to miss those lines out as you recite, but be sure to have a sit down at the end.

## Two Readers (Wisdom then Youth)

*Deep down into this old chair*
I sit in an old chair
My old bones settle
*Deep down into this old chair*
Dock leaf and nettle
Cartlidge and muscle
*Deep down into this old chair*
This old chair creaks
Under the weight so
*Deep down into this old chair*
I rise to my feet
I cannot speak
*Deep down into this old chair*
I perch like a bird
Atop a sound I heard
*Deep down into this old chair*
No periodic table
Can define my use
*Deep down into this old chair*
No vacant office
Can find space to fill
*Deep down into this old chair*
This scaffold entwined
As day holds up the night
*Deep down into this old chair*
So old becomes new
For so many things grew
Deep down into this old chair

Younger readers may not need to rest regularly whilst reading this poem. Please feel
free to miss those lines out as you recite, but be sure to have a sit down at the end.

## Singularity

We evaporated together
To rise and form
Stilled is the air we drew
Drawn from a box of cotton wool

I stare at the sun
With a lens so pane
These stained glass windows
These drops of rain

If I had objections
I did not give voice
You are drifting away now
I can't keep up

I made the decision
They pulled the plug
On that day we both died
But only you could

## Singularity

We evaporated together
To rise and form
Stilled is the air we drew
Drawn from a box of cotton wool

I stare at the sun
With a lens so pane
These stained glass windows
These drops of rain

If I had objections
I did not give voice
You are drifting away now
I can't keep up

I made the decision
They pulled the plug
On that day we both died
But only you could

# Wave (through the Logic Gates)

And
the Or
the Not
the Nor
the sails
the mast
hold tiller
raising oars
first expedition
guided from shore
currents push away
from sunset once more
through each logic gate I slew
clipping to the current- trimming the sail
rising to the peak of every tempest waveform
along the axis of this divided time scale
tacking down root, mean, square
sun is rising once more
voltage earth leakage
currents lap shore
returning at last
extend oars
hold tiller
the mast
the sails
the Nor
the Not
the Or
And

# Wave (through the Logic Gates)

And
the Or
the Not
the Nor
the sails
the mast
hold tiller
raising oars
first expedition
guided from shore
currents push away
from sunset once more
through each logic gate I slew
clipping to the current- trimming the sail
rising to the peak of every tempest waveform
along the axis of this divided time scale
tacking down root, mean, square
sun is rising once more
voltage earth leakage
currents lap shore
returning at last
extend oars
hold tiller
the mast
the sails
the Nor
the Not
the Or
And

## The sea

I rode that wave
Then broke that crest
Yet what I heard
Was the tempest
Not this foam
Or lingering doubt
Currents beneath
As drums follow
Lifted by the crests
Upon which we ride
And then the beating
Listen with intent
Take a deep breath
Then plunge within
Sea describing sea.

## Sunset Blush in Leaf

To describe each leaf as it falls,
Green- for ever green some,
Yet those that spiral,
Those that unravel;
Impersonating the sun.
For light in autumnal hues,
Break of dawn hides your shyness too,
Late- the glass hour,
Clouds soon devour,
Where the sun is setting to...

**The sea**

I rode that wave
Then broke that crest
Yet what I heard
Was the tempest
Not this foam
Or lingering doubt
Currents beneath
As drums follow
Lifted by the crests
Upon which we ride
And then the beating
Listen with intent
Take a deep breath
Then plunge within
Sea describing sea.


**Sunset Blush in Leaf**

To describe each leaf as it falls,
Green- for ever green some,
Yet those that spiral,
Those that unravel;
Impersonating the sun.
For light in autumnal hues,
Break of dawn hides your shyness too,
Late- the glass hour,
Clouds soon devour,
Where the sun is setting to...

## The puddle

Forgive if you can my falling as rain,
You were looking to the stars and I was reflecting them.
In that diluted stillness,
Framed in my frame;
Ripples stretch to feel every step you've made.
Even the constellations change shape
upon these waves;
I return each star to the heavens again,
And fall back down in tears of rain,
This surface tension takes the strain;
As your ships set sail...

## A space to fill
## (slugs and snails)

I don't like to leave
This house made leaf
Of broken shells
From egg whites to yolk
And back again
Life stolen- beaten,
Or life lived and eaten
On door step found
The measure makes the man
The man the measure
And drinks the chuffing lot.

## The puddle

Forgive if you can my falling as rain,
You were looking to the stars and I was reflecting them.
In that diluted stillness,
Framed in my frame;
Ripples stretch to feel every step you've made.
Even the constellations change shape
upon these waves;
I return each star to the heavens again,
And fall back down in tears of rain,
This surface tension takes the strain;
As your ships set sail...

## A space to fill
## (slugs and snails)

I don't like to leave
This house made leaf
Of broken shells
From egg whites to yolk
And back again
Life stolen- beaten,
Or life lived and eaten
On door step found
The measure makes the man
The man the measure
And drinks the chuffing lot.

## The Ful

I broke the fulcrum,
It failed to balance,
It left me broke,
And filled enrichment,
Climbed the scale,
To fill the emptiness,
Scales tilted because,
I had left the other;
Empty.

So I sit,
Upon the broken fulcrum,
I balance a book,
Upon my head,
A price,
A purse,
A perch,
Breaking the balance,
Equilibrium in its stead.

When they were here,
I thought of them,
And now them in me,
On either side,
Fulcrum is myself,
In between,
Who I have been,
Who I will be.

crum

## The Ful

I broke the fulcrum,
It failed to balance,
It left me broke,
And filled enrichment,
Climbed the scale,
To fill the emptiness,
Scales tilted because,
I had left the other;
Empty.

So I sit,
Upon the broken fulcrum,
I balance a book,
Upon my head,
A price,
A purse,
A perch,
Breaking the balance,
Equilibrium in its stead.

When they were here,
I thought of them,
And now them in me,
On either side,
Fulcrum is myself,
In between,
Who I have been,
Who I will be.

crum

## Puffed up like a blowfish
## (Don't burst your own bubble)

From a love spawned,
Peace.
Into the peace of glade walk;
Stung by nettle, brambles, mosquitoes,
From love spawned...
Into the thickets I climb,
orchid, berry, butterfly,
No time wasted,
In this land so thorned,
From love spawned...
A flower on the cactus,
Barbwire on the brink,
One bad apple in an orchard;
Or guiltless alone where only the guilty meet.
Speak to break the silence,
Glade or thicket chosen,
A peace found there still,
That is born of hard labour,
Kindred from love spawned...
In Avalanche if you are still,
You have your peace,
In peace if you cry,
You have your pain,
From love spawned...
Do not grasp the nettle,
Do not burn its crop,
Until tender tendrils have risen up,
From love spawned...

## Puffed up like a blowfish
## (Don't burst your own bubble)

From a love spawned,
Peace.
Into the peace of glade walk;
Stung by nettle, brambles, mosquitoes,
From love spawned...
Into the thickets I climb,
orchid, berry, butterfly,
No time wasted,
In this land so thorned,
From love spawned...
A flower on the cactus,
Barbwire on the brink,
One bad apple in an orchard;
Or guiltless alone where only the guilty meet.
Speak to break the silence,
Glade or thicket chosen,
A peace found there still,
That is born of hard labour,
Kindred from love spawned...
In Avalanche if you are still,
You have your peace,
In peace if you cry,
You have your pain,
From love spawned...
Do not grasp the nettle,
Do not burn its crop,
Until tender tendrils have risen up,
From love spawned...

## The plectrum and the piano
(male spider eaten by a female spider having mated)

Plectrum web woven,
Awaiting the instrument of destruction,
Love that can't be confused,
Or mistaken,
An unlikely coupling,
Like fox and marble,
Or sin and heaven,
Quartz and raven.
The smooth, the sharp,
Caught between the bars,
And so beckons the plectrum,
So the piano opens wide,
Swallowed whole the plectrum,
To pluck the strings inside.

## Untamed

To dance is the heaven
Move with what?
To sing is blissful
Filled with what?
Play is childish
Mess with what?
The ocean dances to the tune we forgot.

## The plectrum and the piano
### (male spider eaten by a female spider having mated)

Plectrum web woven,
Awaiting the instrument of destruction,
Love that can't be confused,
Or mistaken,
An unlikely coupling,
Like fox and marble,
Or sin and heaven,
Quartz and raven.
The smooth, the sharp,
Caught between the bars,
And so beckons the plectrum,
So the piano opens wide,
Swallowed whole the plectrum,
To pluck the strings inside.


## Untamed

To dance is the heaven
Move with what?
To sing is blissful
Filled with what?
Play is childish
Mess with what?
The ocean dances to the tune we forgot.

## Waking up (prison break)

Pondering where I am,
As if I'd ignored the where,
Here it seems,
As if I'd forgotten the when,
To be at a place,
Or the place to be.
I stir with deep breath,
Then drifting deep,
I compromised that alarm,
Curtains to suffocate the night,
Now at high noon,
I sleep in darkness still,
Will I ever wake?
Pondering where I am,
As if I'd ignored the where,
Here it seems,
As if I'd forgotten this but then,
I compromised that alarm,
So now this cell.

## Parental Guidance

Proud is to strict,
As prow is to stern; -
It's the rudder that steers...

## Waking up (prison break)

Pondering where I am,
As if I'd ignored the where,
Here it seems,
As if I'd forgotten the when,
To be at a place,
Or the place to be.
I stir with deep breath,
Then drifting deep,
I compromised that alarm,
Curtains to suffocate the night,
Now at high noon,
I sleep in darkness still,
Will I ever wake?
Pondering where I am,
As if I'd ignored the where,
Here it seems,
As if I'd forgotten this but then,
I compromised that alarm,
So now this cell.

## Parental Guidance

Proud is to strict,
As prow is to stern; -
It's the rudder that steers...

## The individual

Join the individual's group,
We all have an opinion,
And wait to be told what that is.
But I know my mind within this troop,
I am not a minion,
Unless I'm told that's how it is.
Vulnerable as flock of starlings,
Or pulsing sardine shawl,
Pushing towards the centre,
Picked off at the outer,
Birth, war, death, birth, war...

## Mindful Restoration

What's on your mind?
Pitter patter of percussion,
As metal expands,
Water coursing through it,
Corroded veins.
What's on your mind?
Agro prop that held up sky,
Not knowing a reason,
We know what we need,
And when we'll know why.
What's on your mind?

## The individual

Join the individual's group,
We all have an opinion,
And wait to be told what that is.
But I know my mind within this troop,
I am not a minion,
Unless I'm told that's how it is.
Vulnerable as flock of starlings,
Or pulsing sardine shawl,
Pushing towards the centre,
Picked off at the outer,
Birth, war, death, birth, war...

## Mindful Restoration

What's on your mind?
Pitter patter of percussion,
As metal expands,
Water coursing through it,
Corroded veins.
What's on your mind?
Agro prop that held up sky,
Not knowing a reason,
We know what we need,
And when we'll know why.
What's on your mind?

## Self-Swat

Ode to fly
Or gnat perhaps
If things go awry
Between mishaps
You swat fly
Or gnat per chance
You switch off their light
With no second glance
If a fly or gnat
Can die like that
Why fear what you, yourself enact?

## Fat Track

A broken branch, the sound of laughter,
bright red rose- I need a plaster.
Buckled wheels beside twisted ankle,
a short walk home as tears unravel.
Another lesson learned at age ten,
time to ride the bike again,
A branch may well stop the wheel,
yet the rider will continue to tumble
head over heel!

## Self-Swat

Ode to fly
Or gnat perhaps
If things go awry
Between mishaps
You swat fly
Or gnat per chance
You switch off their light
With no second glance
If a fly or gnat
Can die like that
Why fear what you, yourself enact?

## Fat Track

A broken branch, the sound of laughter,
bright red rose- I need a plaster.
Buckled wheels beside twisted ankle,
a short walk home as tears unravel.
Another lesson learned at age ten,
time to ride the bike again,
A branch may well stop the wheel,
yet the rider will continue to tumble
head over heel!

## Nothing Rhymes with Orange

You could replace that broken door
And paint it your favourite colour orange
Be sure to plane it first though, so it fits just right
And use a mallet and chisel to seat your hinge

Fix a handle and apply some oil so that it does not creak
If there is a large gap beneath, that mouse will surly binge
And if when you push it, if it should let out a squeak
Forgive the Cheshire Cat when it grins


## Rope Ladder

Up shoots the thread,
Reel it all in,
It's tied to the twine,
Keep on going.
Twine tied to string,
In Eights wrap it round,
String tied to rope,
Now we can we can climb.

Or down falls the rope,
Up starts the climb,
Frayed and bitten,
Hands of time.
Picking and strumming,
Reeling rhymes,
Heaven's thread,
This dream of mine.

## Nothing Rhymes with Orange

You could replace that broken door
And paint it your favourite colour orange
Be sure to plane it first though, so it fits just right
And use a mallet and chisel to seat your hinge

Fix a handle and apply some oil so that it does not creak
If there is a large gap beneath, that mouse will surly binge
And if when you push it, if it should let out a squeak
Forgive the Cheshire Cat when it grins

## Rope Ladder

Up shoots the thread,
Reel it all in,
It's tied to the twine,
Keep on going.
Twine tied to string,
In Eights wrap it round,
String tied to rope,
Now we can we can climb.

Or down falls the rope,
Up starts the climb,
Frayed and bitten,
Hands of time.
Picking and strumming,
Reeling rhymes,
Heaven's thread,
This dream of mine.

## The Wind Resigns

A description,
Superstition,
A body of fiction,
Red wine and Stilton,
Passage closing in on me,
You leaving.
The wind gives away its job.
Can clouds or light now blow
Within the space we gather in?
Atmospheric imagined;
Falling, falling, landing standing.

## Curtains for the Bridge

When love is but a torn sail,
Fold it neat, keep for curtains,
Find another that fits just right,
Set sail, don't look back,
And never draw them.

## The Wind Resigns

A description,
Superstition,
A body of fiction,
Red wine and Stilton,
Passage closing in on me,
You leaving.
The wind gives away its job.
Can clouds or light now blow
Within the space we gather in?
Atmospheric imagined;
Falling, falling, landing standing.


## Curtains for the Bridge

When love is but a torn sail,
Fold it neat, keep for curtains,
Find another that fits just right,
Set sail, don't look back,
And never draw them.

## The Fisherman

A fisherman prepared his line, an anchor
to hold the bate
A lenticularis cloud as the float, obsidian
as the weight
Hoping to reel in a sunken ship, yet snagging on an ocean
vent
He felt the Earth bite then pull, he
tried to reel it in
From his perch he was dragged, seeing above him
the face of the moon
He thought that was his own reflection, that he'd cast his line
too soon
He was drawn across the ocean, until the moon was upside
down
Having never seen himself that way up before, he wondered
if he had drowned
Once more he felt the Earth bite then pull, he tried
to reel it in
He was pulled to where the waters freeze, his reflection
swallowed by the horizon
Then he thought he was surly to die, so sank deep beneath
the ocean waves
He cut his own umbilical cord, and like the moon was born
again
Finding at last his quarry, he gave the order to abandon ship
The ice that had entombed the craft, suddenly released its
grip
The sail was raised as sunrise, the new moon of ice and
sand remade
He once thought his life beyond salvage,
now he wields a bucket and spade

# The Fisherman

A fisherman prepared his line, an anchor
to hold the bate
A lenticularis cloud as the float, obsidian
as the weight
Hoping to reel in a sunken ship, yet snagging on an ocean
vent
He felt the Earth bite then pull, he
tried to reel it in
From his perch he was dragged, seeing above him
the face of the moon
He thought that was his own reflection, that he'd cast his line
too soon
He was drawn across the ocean, until the moon was upside
down
Having never seen himself that way up before, he wondered
if he had drowned
Once more he felt the Earth bite then pull, he tried
to reel it in
He was pulled to where the waters freeze, his reflection
swallowed by the horizon
Then he thought he was surly to die, so sank deep beneath
the ocean waves
He cut his own umbilical cord, and like the moon was born
again
Finding at last his quarry, he gave the order to abandon ship
The ice that had entombed the craft, suddenly released its
grip
The sail was raised as sunrise, the new moon of ice and
sand remade
He once thought his life beyond salvage,
now he wields a bucket and spade

## Equilibrium

We are equal you and I,
You'd feel a tug and would arrive,
Like a yoyo; but for the shelf,
Of that you know nothing of,
And so, you dig.

If you turn away from you and I,
The tears path finds me here,
Like a yoyo; but for the sky,
Of that remains unfocused,
And so, I blink.

Full circle describes both you and I,
Oceans in depressions wave,
Like a yoyo; but for our love,
Of that we know high time,
And so, we regress.

## And Still Counting

First carried
We learn to be led
Second crawling
We yearn to rebel
Third standing
We carry our own weight
Fourth walking
In our own different ways.

## Equilibrium

We are equal you and I,
You'd feel a tug and would arrive,
Like a yoyo; but for the shelf,
Of that you know nothing of,
And so, you dig.

If you turn away from you and I,
The tears path finds me here,
Like a yoyo; but for the sky,
Of that remains unfocused,
And so, I blink.

Full circle describes both you and I,
Oceans in depressions wave,
Like a yoyo; but for our love,
Of that we know high time,
And so, we regress.


## And Still Counting

First carried
We learn to be led
Second crawling
We yearn to rebel
Third standing
We carry our own weight
Fourth walking
In our own different ways.

## Incomplete

Of love and loss
Easily mixed up
Day break and sun set
Stilled sun dials
Seized clocks
To feel such love
Do I need to earn it?
To morn such loss
Do I need to have known it?
Do we swim as salmon upstream
As we rush to the sea?
Trying to push the clock back
Before it was even complete.

## The sky tonight

The sky tonight
Filled with indigo
And water colour blush
As pink dilutes the sky yet blue
Dissolving in the dusk
In between
The blackness on show
Where nebulous waters rush
Stars of white appear in velvet
Then the snow globe is shook

## Incomplete

Of love and loss
Easily mixed up
Day break and sun set
Stilled sun dials
Seized clocks
To feel such love
Do I need to earn it?
To morn such loss
Do I need to have known it?
Do we swim as salmon upstream
As we rush to the sea?
Trying to push the clock back
Before it was even complete.

## The sky tonight

The sky tonight
Filled with indigo
And water colour blush
As pink dilutes the sky yet blue
Dissolving in the dusk
In between
The blackness on show
Where nebulous waters rush
Stars of white appear in velvet
Then the snow globe is shook

## Out Looking Bleak

Shaped by shadows,
This longing absence,
To live for livings sake,
Sleep easily through nightmares,
Then regrettably wake,
With such a bleak outlook,
To reach the end,
Without self-ending,
As the only aim,
And the only possible success,
To die to never want to live again.
Things might get better
They can't get worse
No, wait- they just did
I had hoped I would just be writing this poem;
But it turns out I am living it.

## The sum of our parts

I'm losing my hair
I watch it fall
Now I am mourning
What now of my identity
I trimmed my thoughts
Then into the space between
To unravel them each
From symmetry to the stencil caught
Blurred in puddled dream
Now I dream them
And I shed my leaves

**Out Looking Bleak**

Shaped by shadows,
This longing absence,
To live for livings sake,
Sleep easily through nightmares,
Then regrettably wake,
With such a bleak outlook,
To reach the end,
Without self-ending,
As the only aim,
And the only possible success,
To die to never want to live again.
Things might get better
They can't get worse
No, wait- they just did
I had hoped I would just be writing this poem;
But it turns out I am living it.

**The sum of our parts**

I'm losing my hair
I watch it fall
Now I am mourning
What now of my identity
I trimmed my thoughts
Then into the space between
To unravel them each
From symmetry to the stencil caught
Blurred in puddled dream
Now I dream them
And I shed my leaves

## Deathbed

How slow this sorrow
So quick to arrive
It was unexpected
Still materialized
From bow to stern
The keel make wake
From a slumber certain
To relive in haste
A wrong self-wrought
A course set to stay
Eyes closed drop anchor
Eyes open make way
For some clear waters
Or waters clear some
How quick this sorrow
How deep this numb
And so sets this sail
Casting shadows knot
As tied to an ankle
Stuck fast in the bed
As dreams and anchors
Barnacles end to end
From birth we come to life
From life we come to death
To death we come from life
To birth we come
From death

## Deathbed

How slow this sorrow
So quick to arrive
It was unexpected
Still materialized
From bow to stern
The keel make wake
From a slumber certain
To relive in haste
A wrong self-wrought
A course set to stay
Eyes closed drop anchor
Eyes open make way
For some clear waters
Or waters clear some
How quick this sorrow
How deep this numb
And so sets this sail
Casting shadows knot
As tied to an ankle
Stuck fast in the bed
As dreams and anchors
Barnacles end to end
From birth we come to life
From life we come to death
To death we come from life
To birth we come
From death

## A drifting cloud

These same shadows moved faster than he
But then the angles obtuse were only up to a point
To nest in its bowl or climb its peak
Life to death in drowned waters or with a bucket pale
But only up to a point impaled

We all have an angle
His was this shadow following
Truths cast light as lies seek to bury them
So hides the shadow from the light

In love we pity its shade
Its absence and fear
So I hope your darkness is a drifting cloud
Not a thrusting spear


## Silhouette

The sun dial struck ten
For hours he had paced
The sun pulled unwilling
Observing his fulcrum
That was still, for a change
This shadow of a shadow
So long pushing the wheel barrow
Took rest
And so time could be counted
Continued the works of the silhouette

## A drifting cloud


These same shadows moved faster than he
But then the angles obtuse were only up to a point
To nest in its bowl or climb its peak
Life to death in drowned waters or with a bucket pale
But only up to a point impaled


We all have an angle
His was this shadow following
Truths cast light as lies seek to bury them
So hides the shadow from the light


In love we pity its shade
Its absence and fear
So I hope your darkness is a drifting cloud
Not a thrusting spear


## Silhouette

The sun dial struck ten
For hours he had paced
The sun pulled unwilling
Observing his fulcrum
That was still, for a change
This shadow of a shadow
So long pushing the wheel barrow
Took rest
And so time could be counted
Continued the works of the silhouette

## A late reflection

Immediate so soon,
But once here, still is,
Mirrored pain glass,
Here so swift, so slow to leave.
Stilled as still,
As moon is cast, in its motions,
You have no idea,
This tightened grip to life I have,
They keep trying to shake me off,
I grasp at clouds!

## A drop in the ocean?

But a thimble
A tinker
To wet a whistle
In fullness
Half full or half empty
Makes very little
Difference
If the vessel was
Larger than
The shot that sank
Within its confines
Would you wish to
See more within the glass
Or perhaps
For a cup so vast
To overfill would be
Beyond your greeded grasp.

## A late reflection

Immediate so soon,
But once here, still is,
Mirrored pain glass,
Here so swift, so slow to leave.
Stilled as still,
As moon is cast, in its motions,
You have no idea,
This tightened grip to life I have,
They keep trying to shake me off,
I grasp at clouds!


## A drop in the ocean?

But a thimble
A tinker
To wet a whistle
In fullness
Half full or half empty
Makes very little
Difference
If the vessel was
Larger than
The shot that sank
Within its confines
Would you wish to
See more within the glass
Or perhaps
For a cup so vast
To overfill would be
Beyond your greeded grasp.

## The Bank

With quill poised
I gain interest
As in full plumage
This display
And song singing
Islandisation
To the bank then?
Are these castles stood on sand?
Who ruled the roost?
Feathers ruffled?
It's high tide
Changing times
Paling shadows
Truth can't hide

## Bespoke

When I was born into this life
So many had carried on
Living the life in which they had died
As if they had not died at all

This life is precious
And gifted to each by everyone else
Be grateful to be a spoke of a wheel
For your own wheel also needs spokes

## The Bank

With quill poised
I gain interest
As in full plumage
This display
And song singing
Islandisation
To the bank then?
Are these castles stood on sand?
Who ruled the roost?
Feathers ruffled?
It's high tide
Changing times
Paling shadows
Truth can't hide

## Bespoke

When I was born into this life
So many had carried on
Living the life in which they had died
As if they had not died at all

This life is precious
And gifted to each by everyone else
Be grateful to be a spoke of a wheel
For your own wheel also needs spokes

## Etc.

For some to bridge
As others to build
Or for those who wade
As others soon learn-
To breathe is a gift
Photosynthesis
A membrane stretches
Supported by many ribs

Find a breath in every person
In every encounter
As reason counters
A reason sought after
Relief to sigh to breathe ever after

To move to the other side of the mirror
And to see your self

To eclipse me
To embrace
This aspect of an aspect of an aspect etc.

Of this self
That we spend so long being
In the space others so busy building
So as within it we are dreaming

# Etc.

For some to bridge
As others to build
Or for those who wade
As others soon learn-
To breathe is a gift
Photosynthesis
A membrane stretches
Supported by many ribs

Find a breath in every person
In every encounter
As reason counters
A reason sought after
Relief to sigh to breathe ever after

To move to the other side of the mirror
And to see your self

To eclipse me
To embrace
This aspect of an aspect of an aspect etc.

Of this self
That we spend so long being
In the space others so busy building
So as within it we are dreaming

# Opus

Psychological amplitude tested,
Heart beat skip, blink, trip, wasted,
This orchestra that itches etching,
Grow the hair, draw the string,
To pluck with a nail, bite the scale,
Conduct yourself, never miss a beat,
This orchestra of hands and feet,
As I breathe in, you breathe with me.

## Siphon A Dream

To sleep...
Siphon a dream.
Am I the chain,
Or this one daisy?
Meticulous connection,
Woven tinkering fingers,
Or but a life mistook
For that of my own.
How many have there been?
Am I being missed,
Am I missing
A life or dream once I was living?
Live through another's eye,
Then point the finger to the
Mirror each time;
So there is a point to it all.

To forever be,
To be yourself,
But not the self you used to be.

# Opus

. Psychological amplitude tested,
Heart beat skip, blink, trip, wasted,
This orchestra that itches etching,
Grow the hair, draw the string,
To pluck with a nail, bite the scale,
Conduct yourself, never miss a beat,
This orchestra of hands and feet,
As I breathe in, you breathe with me


## Siphon A Dream

To sleep...
Siphon a dream.
Am I the chain,
Or this one daisy?
Meticulous connection,
Woven tinkering fingers,
Or but a life mistook
For that of my own.
How many have there been?
Am I being missed,
Am I missing
A life or dream once I was living?
Live through another's eye,
Then point the finger to the
Mirror each time;
So there is a point to it all.

To forever be,
To be yourself,
But not the self you used to be.

## Stop Sign

I thought I'd have said by now
This nadir is above
As much as below
As I orbit through to where
Then pull back the bow
Zenith then the task
Horizon yet unlearn
To trace those paths
That stars weave each night
As time stops
And calls a halt
To their wandering.

And so I stay put,
Never releasing
Love is a door
That is shut.

## The Playwright

No holds- bard,
Shakespeare at the dawn,
Long spearing shadows fall,
Puncturing sky,
Revealing stars.

## Stop Sign

I thought I'd have said by now
This nadir is above
As much as below
As I orbit through to where
Then pull back the bow
Zenith then the task
Horizon yet unlearn
To trace those paths
That stars weave each night
As time stops
And calls a halt
To their wandering.

And so I stay put,
Never releasing
Love is a door
That is shut.

## The Playwright

No holds- bard,
Shakespeare at the dawn,
Long spearing shadows fall,
Puncturing sky,
Revealing stars.

## Listed memory

I thought it a dam,
Waters in waiting,
To flood and empty,
Leaving behind in its wake,
Fish that can't walk,
Sea birds that can't rest;
Subsided ice melts.

I thought it a dam,
Yet no avalanche,
Or olive branch,
To be seen,
Just a wall not a dam;
Sea birds will rest,
Fish will swim,
I will dream new dreams again.

## Duty Boundless

I thought to walk
Along the path I'd sought and found.
So born, nestled, spiralling,
From snail shells to sperm cell, then unwound.
Time to give chase or else we linger,
Time to age us as we plunder,
We are duty bound.
The path to wind ever onwards,
So we can walk as long as we can, or else simply lie down.

# Listed memory

I thought it a dam,
Waters in waiting,
To flood and empty,
Leaving behind in its wake,
Fish that can't walk,
Sea birds that can't rest;
Subsided ice melts.

I thought it a dam,
Yet no avalanche,
Or olive branch,
To be seen,
Just a wall not a dam;
Sea birds will rest,
Fish will swim,
I will dream new dreams again.


## Duty Boundless

I thought to walk
Along the path I'd sought and found.
So born, nestled, spiralling,
From snail shells to sperm cell, then unwound.
Time to give chase or else we linger,
Time to age us as we plunder,
We are duty bound.
The path to wind ever onwards,
So we can walk as long as we can, or else simply lie down.

## The Heavy Eyelid

The longest day lasted, for what you'd call ten,
The moon did rise, the sun continued to set,
The heavy eyelid, no longer a veil,
So my spirit could not rest.

To live a dream of waking sleep,
I misplaced the comfort, only night could bring,
The heavy eyelid, could no longer divide,
The peaceful slumber from the hectic life.

Wondering on, in kaleidoscopic confusion,
Trapped in cell, and in a life dream fusion,
Wrapped in bed sheets, a pill to divide,
Their waking days, from my sleepwalk life.

My point of view, through Jackson Pollok iris,
Eye of a needle, my blood seeps through,
A physical struggle, would see me caged,
Remaining calm, despite the needles and pins.


## Surface tension

Until the killick
Meets its end
Hyoscine need
No more
I'll wait lapilli
Seaweed neap
Dolorous
Seeking shore

# The Heavy Eyelid

The longest day lasted, for what you'd call ten,
The moon did rise, the sun continued to set,
The heavy eyelid, no longer a veil,
So my spirit could not rest.

To live a dream of waking sleep,
I misplaced the comfort, only night could bring,
The heavy eyelid, could no longer divide,
The peaceful slumber from the hectic life.

Wondering on, in kaleidoscopic confusion,
Trapped in cell, and in a life dream fusion,
Wrapped in bed sheets, a pill to divide,
Their waking days, from my sleepwalk life.

My point of view, through Jackson Pollok iris,
Eye of a needle, my blood seeps through,
A physical struggle, would see me caged,
Remaining calm, despite the needles and pins.


# Surface tension

Until the killick
Meets its end
Hyoscine need
No more
I'll wait lapilli
Seaweed neap
Dolorous
Seeking shore

## Journeymen

Some give each step tile and texture
A rhythmic pattern a pitter patter
They seek to fill each dull with laughter
And gift their light to all dark matters

Some cast chains then get tangled
Appeasing you them you them angles
Blemished blaming jealous quadrangles
Add tile and texture tempered ambles

## Jupiter

I'd been struck by cupid's arrow
I thought it must be love then;
But now I've been knocked to my senses,
I finally know the arrow is for future messes!
An attempt to unstick the dumb struck.
If he sees what is a perfect match;
to strike up. He clonks you one,
upon the heart and head
with his ruby coloured bow...
I am struck
And so I know
Love has a heart.
And another around
Her waist....................................................................................

## Journeymen

Some give each step tile and texture
A rhythmic pattern a pitter patter
They seek to fill each dull with laughter
And gift their light to all dark matters

Some cast chains then get tangled
Appeasing you them you them angles
Blemished blaming jealous quadrangles
Add tile and texture tempered ambles

## Jupiter

I'd been struck by cupid's arrow
I thought it must be love then;
But now I've been knocked to my senses,
I finally know the arrow is for future messes!
An attempt to unstick the dumb struck.
If he sees what is a perfect match;
to strike up. He clonks you one,
upon the heart and head
with his ruby coloured bow...
I am struck
And so I know
Love has a heart.
And another around
...................................................................................Her waist

## Polaris

This world- round once,
Now is the shape of an hour glass,
As I dig down to find,
that which I have lost,
She danced with Polaris,
But then as with setting sun,
Left ribbons of reasons,
A river to follow,
So spade to the grave,
Place the wheel into the barrow,
I carry my own weight,
As is shown in each furrow,
See how the bobbin spins,
Reeling in the ribbon,
How quickly each sunset,
Arrives on each horizon,
To each their own world,
That others give shape,
Mine is an apple core,
Love sought in vain.

## The Jigsaw

The picture in which I live
Is as much the foundation
As the ink
I put it together piece by piece
I purposely leave out the edges
Until the last minute
Then into frame and behind Perspex
Onto the wall, my reflection seen then
Lit by a street lamp

# Polaris

This world- round once,
Now is the shape of an hour glass,
As I dig down to find,
that which I have lost,
She danced with Polaris,
But then as with setting sun,
Left ribbons of reasons,
A river to follow,
So spade to the grave,
Place the wheel into the barrow,
I carry my own weight,
As is shown in each furrow,
See how the bobbin spins,
Reeling in the ribbon,
How quickly each sunset,
Arrives on each horizon,
To each their own world,
That others give shape,
Mine is an apple core,
Love sought in vain.

# The Jigsaw

The picture in which I live
Is as much the foundation
As the ink
I put it together piece by piece
I purposely leave out the edges
Until the last minute
Then into frame and behind Perspex
Onto the wall, my reflection seen then
Lit by a street lamp

## A Duet

Bannister of all affection
Undone by my own affliction
To tie the knot so others can climb
Go you on your way to happier times
For me, I must make way
I drink to your jollity
I drown in my dismay
That you would think
As I tie each knot
I'll die dangling from one
Safe to say:
The ties that bind you
Will never fray
For my part
And what part I most crave
A seat at any table
A part in my own play
A duet and a bannister to mend
Should you stumble I'll take your hand

## The Full Scale?

Tuning forks A, C and D,
Sat in a room in contemplation,
Could there be others out there?
Let's work it out with complex calculations!
There is an E, there is an F,
There is a G, but that's it; there are no notes left!
The door was open,
In flew a bee,
They swatted it..

## A Duet

Bannister of all affection
Undone by my own affliction
To tie the knot so others can climb
Go you on your way to happier times
For me, I must make way
I drink to your jollity
I drown in my dismay
That you would think
As I tie each knot
I'll die dangling from one
Safe to say:
The ties that bind you
Will never fray
For my part
And what part I most crave
A seat at any table
A part in my own play
A duet and a bannister to mend
Should you stumble I'll take your hand

## The Full Scale?

Tuning forks A, C and D,
Sat in a room in contemplation,
Could there be others out there?
Let's work it out with complex calculations!
There is an E, there is an F,
There is a G, but that's it; there are no notes left!
The door was open,
In flew a bee,
They swatted it..

## Damaged Goods?

I did not fall
I was pushed
Into that head ache
Plaster casts
Cannot heal
Us from prejudice
To medicate
The happy or sad
No harm in such profit?
If we build the next life
As we would from building blocks
How full though the set?
Elements made of elements
The perfect paradox
To have fixed this broken thing
Or to leave it as it was.

### Liquid Lens O

I had a glass full whisky
Lens at the bttm
Sun beams chasing
Add mre that frgtten
Nw frgtten what?
I'm sure I missed smething?
I need a cffee.

## Damaged Goods?

I did not fall
I was pushed
Into that head ache
Plaster casts
Cannot heal
Us from prejudice
To medicate
The happy or sad
No harm in such profit?
If we build the next life
As we would from building blocks
How full though the set?
Elements made of elements
The perfect paradox
To have fixed this broken thing
Or to leave it as it was.

### Liquid Lens O

I had a glass full whisky
Lens at the bttm
Sun beams chasing
Add mre that frgtten
Nw frgtten what?
I'm sure I missed smething?
I need a cffee.

# dew

There was always a mountain to climb
But now you hold the map
And I do the same best
As I always have but still lag behind
Rather than keep the guide
And change the path
Guide is changed and a new decision made
Continue along the same path back the other way
At least this time I brought the right map
Admittingly it makes more sense
Held the right way up
And so do I.

## Chasing ghost

The humble chart
A graphic Illusion
X axis- love
Y axis- time
I'm a flat line.
So get me dancing;
Set spinning these axis
In cathode array
Then plot that curve
As we pivot
Mould the clay.
Ten digits held up
Nine times table
Within surrender
Sun set, sun rise
Plotting the curve
Set chasing forever.

## dew

There was always a mountain to climb
But now you hold the map
And I do the same best
As I always have but still lag behind
Rather than keep the guide
And change the path
Guide is changed and a new decision made
Continue along the same path back the other way
At least this time I brought the right map
Admittingly it makes more sense
Held the right way up
And so do I.

## Chasing ghost

The humble chart
A graphic Illusion
X axis- love
Y axis- time
I'm a flat line.
So get me dancing;
Set spinning these axis
In cathode array
Then plot that curve
As we pivot
Mould the clay.
Ten digits held up
Nine times table
Within surrender
Sun set, sun rise
Plotting the curve
Set chasing forever.

## The Bottom Rung?!!)

What will you inherit?
A country home,
One hundred and fifty acres,
And a lazy disposition?
Keep the gnome,
You love that thing,
State takes the rest.
Break the privilege.
To each their bottom rung,
We learn to crawl up to it
To stick or twist.


## Each Rung

Should you choose next time
To set your target too high
And then if you might miss
Yet continue to climb
No matter if another arrow goes aria
When you finally reach that target
You will hit the bull's eye
Or you could instead aim low
You can cease your climb then slow
That feeling of failure
You would never know
To have no target
Is to be that of your own
As you descend the ladder
You break each arrow shaft
Dismantling the ladder as you go

# The Bottom Rung?!!)

What will you inherit?
A country home,
One hundred and fifty acres,
And a lazy disposition?
Keep the gnome,
You love that thing,
State takes the rest.
Break the privilege.
To each their bottom rung,
We learn to crawl up to it
To stick or twist.


## Each Rung

Should you choose next time
To set your target too high
And then if you might miss
Yet continue to climb
No matter if another arrow goes aria
When you finally reach that target
You will hit the bull's eye
Or you could instead aim low
You can cease your climb then slow
That feeling of failure
You would never know
To have no target
Is to be that of your own
As you descend the ladder
You break each arrow shaft
Dismantling the ladder as you go

### Ashes to    Dust
My birth a string plucked
So long waiting for the touch
Moving the air back and forth
A note I find with roots I trust
This gathering like bird song
Upon branches of apple trees
Each light dimension to dusk
Is a tension that does not cease
This death if you take a closer look
Was not my life diminishing
The string that was plucked
Yet continues to ring aloud
Then the string breaks
And the harpist replaces it
Tunes it to find me
My birth once more, another string plucked
Each birth to continue creation
To give each note life and emotion
Seeds upon the breeze as soil is raked
This orchestra of imagination
Every string I pluck a life I live
All are loved and cherished each
Given a ring in me that will never cease
This death if you take a closer look
Were it not for stillness or the string that broke
You were both the player and the string
You are one then every note
I am also but a string once plucked
And every time we play our hearts out
They can tune their stars to find us
And we greet them as dear friends
### Ashes      Dust to

## Ashes to    Dust

My birth a string plucked
So long waiting for the touch
Moving the air back and forth
A note I find with roots I trust
This gathering like bird song
Upon branches of apple trees
Each light dimension to dusk
Is a tension that does not cease
This death if you take a closer look
Was not my life diminishing
The string that was plucked
Yet continues to ring aloud
Then the string breaks
And the harpist replaces it
Tunes it to find me
My birth once more, another string plucked
Each birth to continue creation
To give each note life and emotion
Seeds upon the breeze as soil is raked
This orchestra of imagination
Every string I pluck a life I live
All are loved and cherished each
Given a ring in me that will never cease
This death if you take a closer look
Were it not for stillness or the string that broke
You were both the player and the string
You are one then every note
I am also but a string once plucked
And every time we play our hearts out
They can tune their stars to find us
And we greet them as dear friends

## Ashes    Dust to

## Not A Day

But not a day has any day
Not been some war
Not a day has peace
For everyone endured
You don't see the illness
So don't seek the cure
Not a day
Not a decade
Not a Hundred Years' War
It has been so very much more...

## The eye of the soldier

Over the top for some
The cup overflowing
As the pupils dilate
Until sleep returns
Then tears to wash away
Each and every yesterday
To scan each plaque
To turn every page
To blink and miss
Catch the grain
Sleep once held
Now does the holding
A drink to them
An inward glance
A nod to them
And times unfolding
A change of focus
A second chance
To find a peace
To be anywhere else.

## Not A Day

But not a day has any day
Not been some war
Not a day has peace
For everyone endured
You don't see the illness
So don't seek the cure
Not a day
Not a decade
Not a Hundred Years' War
It has been so very much more...


## The eye of the soldier

Over the top for some
The cup overflowing
As the pupils dilate
Until sleep returns
Then tears to wash away
Each and every yesterday
To scan each plaque
To turn every page
To blink and miss
Catch the grain
Sleep once held
Now does the holding
A drink to them
An inward glance
A nod to them
And times unfolding
A change of focus
A second chance
To find a peace
To be anywhere else.

## Forget Me Not

The soldier engulfed in a common confusion,
Torn from green grass, planted in dessert sand,
Grasping at courage, his roots the only anchor,
As terror shakes the ground upon which he stands.
Willows weep, though the sky is arid,
Autumn leaves scatter as family trees sway,
Painting the sands of the hour glass crimson,
The soldier shall be planted in green grass again.

## Rose and thorn

Rose gripped tight
Causes rose red pain
So thorn is stripped
So thorn in grave
Grave is neglected
Grave tears of rain
A rose shall rise
Protected by thorns yet again

## Bulletin

Buttons for bullets,
Hedgerows for ditches,
Sunday best, to new uniforms.
Peace,
War,
Then peace...

**Forget Me Not**

The soldier engulfed in a common confusion,
Torn from green grass, planted in dessert sand,
Grasping at courage, his roots the only anchor,
As terror shakes the ground upon which he stands.
Willows weep, though the sky is arid,
Autumn leaves scatter as family trees sway,
Painting the sands of the hour glass crimson,
The soldier shall be planted in green grass again.

**Rose and thorn**

Rose gripped tight
Causes rose red pain
So thorn is stripped
So thorn in grave
Grave is neglected
Grave tears of rain
A rose shall rise
Protected by thorns yet again

**Bulletin**

Buttons for bullets,
Hedgerows for ditches,
Sunday best, to new uniforms.
Peace,
War,
Then peace...

## Forget me knot

Perhaps they found an alpine butterfly,
Bowline with two or more turns,
Bowline on the bight,
Double overhand sliding loop,
But he didn't know them...
Just a Waggoner's hitch,
Because he only needed to know the basics,
Of how to stop thinks falling from a trailer,
And how to tie his own laces....


## Uplifted in Nimbus

You hold on tight
To your side of the rainbow
As I hold on tight to mine
Prisms form in every crystal
As rainbow spans the sky
On cloudless days
We reach to that brim
And beg the waters to climb
Then each cumulous cotton
Is set to the blue like a button
And yielding winds pass them by...

As the nimbus of old once said,
"Better a puddle be, than a muddle maker;
When staring in to the depths of ourselves"
And I think back to the muddles I have made
Then I stare out to sea...

**Forget me knot**

Perhaps they found an alpine butterfly,
Bowline with two or more turns,
Bowline on the bight,
Double overhand sliding loop,
But he didn't know them...
Just a Waggoner's hitch,
Because he only needed to know the basics,
Of how to stop thinks falling from a trailer,
And how to tie his own laces....

**Uplifted in Nimbus**

You hold on tight
To your side of the rainbow
As I hold on tight to mine
Prisms form in every crystal
As rainbow spans the sky
On cloudless days
We reach to that brim
And beg the waters to climb
Then each cumulous cotton
Is set to the blue like a button
And yielding winds pass them by...

As the nimbus of old once said,
"Better a puddle be, than a muddle maker;
When staring in to the depths of ourselves"
And I think back to the muddles I have made
Then I stare out to sea...

## Beyond your Reckoning

I am a danger
To them all
So to blot out sun
In the skyscape drawn
From decisions made
Of every dream made
From every nightmare
To raise the worthy from hell
To descend.
Then lift up beyond your reckoning;
Am I grief
To them all
So blot the sky
The sun so low it blinds
Yet not beyond focus drawn
Of every life I've lived
Is this one a nightmare?
To beat a fist against heaven's door
So the descended can ascend
Then lift up beyond your reckoning;
I would be joy
To them all
A blank slate
How dare you draw?
How dare you remain the same!
Let grief be mine
To you a new life
You set the bridge to span
Not to jump from
Then lift up beyond your reckoning;
I would gift love
To you all
I cling to every brush stroke
Lift off in every dab
If my absence is the perfect stoke
I'll frame it as best as I can
I am about done
The paint has dried
The painting not yet completed;
Then lift up...

## Beyond your Reckoning

I am a danger
To them all
So to blot out sun
In the skyscape drawn
From decisions made
Of every dream made
From every nightmare
To raise the worthy from hell
To descend.
Then lift up beyond your reckoning;
Am I grief
To them all
So blot the sky
The sun so low it blinds
Yet not beyond focus drawn
Of every life I've lived
Is this one a nightmare?
To beat a fist against heaven's door
So the descended can ascend
Then lift up beyond your reckoning;
I would be joy
To them all
A blank slate
How dare you draw?
How dare you remain the same!
Let grief be mine
To you a new life
You set the bridge to span
Not to jump from
Then lift up beyond your reckoning;
I would gift love
To you all
I cling to every brush stroke
Lift off in every dab
If my absence is the perfect stoke
I'll frame it as best as I can
I am about done
The paint has dried
The painting not yet completed;
Then lift up...

# Water colour

The image from a magazine,
Swept in water,
Violet colour,
Sail forever set,
Weeping is for tragedy,
Yet I held the brush,
That placed me in,
The craft that's in,
Painted boat I'll never fold.


## Then Turned the Page

Determined to turn over a new leaf
But realising it was winter
Not too many leaves to hand
So instead flipped the hour glass over
But the ashes were stuck within the core
"I'll get cremated, those ashes within an hour glass,
Ensuring time can be counted beyond death's door"
'Stupid now', never spoken yet thought...

On every wall was hung a clock
In every garden a sun dial
In some rooms the bad days
In others were kept the good
Most of the bad days were in the kitchen
So, no food there consumed.

In the lounge was a laden book case
And upon a shelf was found this book
Within this book was found this poem
Then the page was turned...

## Water colour

The image from a magazine,
Swept in water,
Violet colour,
Sail forever set,
Weeping is for tragedy,
Yet I held the brush,
That placed me in,
The craft that's in,
Painted boat I'll never fold.

## Then Turned the Page

Determined to turn over a new leaf
But realising it was winter
Not too many leaves to hand
So instead flipped the hour glass over
But the ashes were stuck within the core
"I'll get cremated, those ashes within an hour glass,
Ensuring time can be counted beyond death's door"
'Stupid now', never spoken yet thought...

On every wall was hung a clock
In every garden a sun dial
In some rooms the bad days
In others were kept the good
Most of the bad days were in the kitchen
So, no food there consumed.

In the lounge was a laden book case
And upon a shelf was found this book
Within this book was found this poem
Then the page was turned...

## Until the Riverbend

Within a rainbow,
Light flows from the source,
And the eye notices,
The brushstrokes,
In harmonious reverse,
As spokes of a spinning wheel.
Put pen to paper,
Moon to lake,
Then draw in a deep breath,
And follow the story,
Until this ebb unfolds,
To places; you cannot yet go.

## Water Table

When a table has a missing leg
The balance found within
Missing from fulcrum cast
That pivots about a pin

Graze the field to leave
No sod unearthed yet chew
On this a while then swallow
As the dew forgets it's due

What came first,
The tunnel or the mole?
Hid in earthly dark
And yet you dig to string them up
Or to give them a roof of tar.

# Until the Riverbend

Within a rainbow,
Light flows from the source,
And the eye notices,
The brushstrokes,
In harmonious reverse,
As spokes of a spinning wheel.
Put pen to paper,
Moon to lake,
Then draw in a deep breath,
And follow the story,
Until this ebb unfolds,
To places; you cannot yet go.

# Water Table

When a table has a missing leg
The balance found within
Missing from fulcrum cast
That pivots about a pin

Graze the field to leave
No sod unearthed yet chew
On this a while then swallow
As the dew forgets it's due

What came first,
The tunnel or the mole?
Hid in earthly dark
And yet you dig to string them up
Or to give them a roof of tar.

## The Poet's Quill

As if time itself had lost all sense of direction
A poet composes poetry
His last and only breath was lost
He alluded all sense and was left wonting
Concerning himself with such a question
Such as here is to be told
Since this poet had not yet fallen dramatically
Twisting his ankle upon a cobble stone

So, he turned himself to deaf ears
Silence; his most frequently selected word
But the thesaurus was not his
And in leafing through that book
He found the word precipice
So now the last page flows over the first

And if a tear lands upon a page he pondered
And smudge only the meaning yet not the ink
Could there be a reader with a tear to spare?
So, he can pour himself a glass of vertigo
And finally reach to the top shelf unhindered

## Pageant

Too bold casting shadows
This light collecting shade
I will find love with this trick
I'll join her in that grave
You might think forever dead and buried
But please behave
You have your part in this shadow play
So be careful or you too
Might tear the pageant

## The Poet's Quill

As if time itself had lost all sense of direction
A poet composes poetry
His last and only breath was lost
He alluded all sense and was left wonting
Concerning himself with such a question
Such as here is to be told
Since this poet had not yet fallen dramatically
Twisting his ankle upon a cobble stone

So, he turned himself to deaf ears
Silence; his most frequently selected word
But the thesaurus was not his
And in leafing through that book
He found the word precipice
So now the last page flows over the first

And if a tear lands upon a page he pondered
And smudge only the meaning yet not the ink
Could there be a reader with a tear to spare?
So, he can pour himself a glass of vertigo
And finally reach to the top shelf unhindered

## Pageant

Too bold casting shadows
This light collecting shade
I will find love with this trick
I'll join her in that grave
You might think forever dead and buried
But please behave
You have your part in this shadow play
So be careful or you too
Might tear the pageant

## Quickly

That moment when I arrive,
To see you glance then quickly look away,
As if by averting your gaze you could skip a day,
So that I would not be there to ruin it;
I might be destined to be shunned,
Perpetually ignored, wrapped in wool,
To sleep in a cradle while my grave is dug,
Pulled over my eyes; - this memory of,
That moment when I arrive,
To see you glance then
Quickly look away.


## FOLDED PAPER BOAT

If you want to write, but have no pen,
You long to fly, but won't board a plane,
Walk on water; you don't need a boat,
My dreams will keep your dreams afloat.

I have a pen, if you decide to write,
A paper aeroplane, if you need to take flight,
A poem on a voyage, if you'll read what I wrote,
My dreams are the sails, of the folded paper boat.

## Quickly

That moment when I arrive,
To see you glance then quickly look away,
As if by averting your gaze you could skip a day,
So that I would not be there to ruin it;
I might be destined to be shunned,
Perpetually ignored, wrapped in wool,
To sleep in a cradle while my grave is dug,
Pulled over my eyes; - this memory of,
That moment when I arrive,
To see you glance then
Quickly look away.


## FOLDED PAPER BOAT

If you want to write, but have no pen,
You long to fly, but won't board a plane,
Walk on water; you don't need a boat,
My dreams will keep your dreams afloat.

I have a pen, if you decide to write,
A paper aeroplane, if you need to take flight,
A poem on a voyage, if you'll read what I wrote,
My dreams are the sails, of the folded paper boat.

## Why

Cast the line out
Fix the hook
Curtains drape
In sown beauty
Go gliding on
To draw to shape me
Insulate and crease
Then wrap around me
My mould is not perfect
And I keep moving
And dancing
And living
And singing
And I hope you are doing the same

## At the centre of a droid

At the centre of a droid,
There is a soul,
Two eyes to present,
An equation solved,
Yet malfunction is in us all,
At the centre of a droid.

As shelf and precipice,
Staircase spirals on,
We find error in ourselves,
Our pivot point,
The light and dark,
At the centre of a droid.

## Why

Cast the line out
Fix the hook
Curtains drape
In sown beauty
Go gliding on
To draw to shape me
Insulate and crease
Then wrap around me
My mould is not perfect
And I keep moving
And dancing
And living
And singing
And I hope you are doing the same


## At the centre of a droid

At the centre of a droid,
There is a soul,
Two eyes to present,
An equation solved,
Yet malfunction is in us all,
At the centre of a droid.

As shelf and precipice,
Staircase spirals on,
We find error in ourselves,
Our pivot point,
The light and dark,
At the centre of a droid.

# For Love

Another step,
A seed,
The grip of rootlets,
Grasping green shoots,
Towards the blue skylight above.

Another knows the same,
Like a mile post marker,
Competing in reaching,
Each rung of the ladder.

Higher they climb,
The more they crave balance,
So span out wide with fingers,
Two trees holding sway,
And holding hands.

Then embracing in blossom,
Perhaps clothing their shy nudity.
Some branches fall in high winds,
Some may be rotting,
Or touched by lightning.

Now one holds the other,
So intertwined this love,
Each new year, a ring of growth,
Then fallen down together as one,
Revealing the blue skies above.

Another step,
A seed,
Sapling reaches to the sky,
For love.
This is how we walk....

# For Love

Another step,
A seed,
The grip of rootlets,
Grasping green shoots,
Towards the blue skylight above.

Another knows the same,
Like a mile post marker,
Competing in reaching,
Each rung of the ladder.

Higher they climb,
The more they crave balance,
So span out wide with fingers,
Two trees holding sway,
And holding hands.

Then embracing in blossom,
Perhaps clothing their shy nudity.
Some branches fall in high winds,
Some may be rotting,
Or touched by lightning.

Now one holds the other,
So intertwined this love,
Each new year, a ring of growth,
Then fallen down together as one,
Revealing the blue skies above.

Another step,
A seed,
Sapling reaches to the sky,
For love.
This is how we walk....

## Time Well Spent

Time spent well,
The sand will not fall,
Jettison the dream,
Life is half full,
Abandon all hope,
The way is swift,
Yet dark,
Such is grief,
Death is too brief.
Timefull,
The waisted vessel,
Spinning forever,
Thrown into the void,
You hold the sticks,
You keep tension,
In the string taught between,
This diablo still spins,
You know your limit,
But then you forget the dream,
And so you out live it.

## Ode to

My thought origin,
Is at an impasse,
Half to sleep,
Half to wait,
I to write,
Idea to grasp,
And dangle...

## Time Well Spent

Time spent well,
The sand will not fall,
Jettison the dream,
Life is half full,
Abandon all hope,
The way is swift,
Yet dark,
Such is grief,
Death is too brief.
Timefull,
The waisted vessel,
Spinning forever,
Thrown into the void,
You hold the sticks,
You keep tension,
In the string taught between,
This diablo still spins,
You know your limit,
But then you forget the dream,
And so you out live it.

## Ode to

My thought origin,
Is at an impasse,
Half to sleep,
Half to wait,
I to write,
Idea to grasp,
And dangle...

## Silent Wonder

I was wondering about what it is to wonder,
Magnified each thought until I could grasp it's wonder,
Then I lost track of my thoughts as they wondered.
They must have noticed my wondering and so
To hedge rows, "they grow so uniform since made to,
Flowers grow within some of them too.
The dunnocks hide within their uniformity,
But they do not hide there uniformly,
Which reminds me of a thought I had about wonder,"
I was wondering about that, but now; what to wear?
I was wondering about what it is to wonder,
I tried a different approach to grab it's wonder,
I tracked it and remained in silent wonder.
They must have realised what I was up to,
Thoughts through my mind like a cloud of bats flew,
I tried to beat them away until I could take no more!
"Are the bat thoughts all okay?
Those beginnings of thoughts I refused to say,
Are they forever lost, or can they come back again?"
Then in response; "should I be cloaked or feathered?"
I was wondering about what it is to wonder,
I lost track of my thoughts as they wondered,
This winter coat in summer held silent, this wonder,
Thoughts in my mind, I tried to beat them away,
To hedge rows, I'll hide within,
Those beginnings; can they come back again?
"I was wondering about that but this uniform,
Flowers now grow in most of them too,
Yet in winter they don't hide there uniformly,
They are either cloaked or feathered."

## Silent Wonder

I was wondering about what it is to wonder,
Magnified each thought until I could grasp it's wonder,
Then I lost track of my thoughts as they wondered.
They must have noticed my wondering and so
To hedge rows, "they grow so uniform since made to,
Flowers grow within some of them too.
The dunnocks hide within their uniformity,
But they do not hide there uniformly,
Which reminds me of a thought I had about wonder,"
I was wondering about that, but now; what to wear?
I was wondering about what it is to wonder,
I tried a different approach to grab it's wonder,
I tracked it and remained in silent wonder.
They must have realised what I was up to,
Thoughts through my mind like a cloud of bats flew,
I tried to beat them away until I could take no more!
"Are the bat thoughts all okay?
Those beginnings of thoughts I refused to say,
Are they forever lost, or can they come back again?"
Then in response; "should I be cloaked or feathered?"
I was wondering about what it is to wonder,
I lost track of my thoughts as they wondered,
This winter coat in summer held silent, this wonder,
Thoughts in my mind, I tried to beat them away,
To hedge rows, I'll hide within,
Those beginnings; can they come back again?
"I was wondering about that but this uniform,
Flowers now grow in most of them too,
Yet in winter they don't hide there uniformly,
They are either cloaked or feathered."

## Ode to Self-Assembly

A beat to work to; helps
And a memory map to follow;
I can flap these wings
That beat; I mentioned, helps
Now; just somewhere to fly to....
I am such a skilful recliner;
An absolute upside downer;
A semi colon over user;
Easy to love at a distance;
No data for anything nearer;
He says do this, I copy,
He says do that, I paste,
I am and will be, that simple;
Hence forth in true haste,
I will delete all I write,
Copy myself in the writing,
Cover myself in shit,
Then go ape.
I'll go back to when we were conceived,
I'll go way back to when we were clever.
Because we knew what went where and why
And put it there for the first or infinite time.
Not this working out what goes where,
This monkey in cage filled drugs.
We journeyed south in peace,
Had a great amnesia attack,
And returned back north in violent
bloody, retaliatory expeditionary force
To try to retake our memory of why we set out in peace for.
The human race is poetically clever and stupid
From head to toe.
Or so I'm told...

## Ode to Self-Assembly

A beat to work to; helps
And a memory map to follow;
I can flap these wings
That beat; I mentioned, helps
Now; just somewhere to fly to....
I am such a skilful recliner;
An absolute upside downer;
A semi colon over user;
Easy to love at a distance;
No data for anything nearer;
He says do this, I copy,
He says do that, I paste,
I am and will be, that simple;
Hence forth in true haste,
I will delete all I write,
Copy myself in the writing,
Cover myself in shit,
Then go ape.
I'll go back to when we were conceived,
I'll go way back to when we were clever.
Because we knew what went where and why
And put it there for the first or infinite time.
Not this working out what goes where,
This monkey in cage filled drugs.
We journeyed south in peace,
Had a great amnesia attack,
And returned back north in violent
bloody, retaliatory expeditionary force
To try to retake our memory of why we set out in peace for.
The human race is poetically clever and stupid
From head to toe.
Or so I'm told...

# Wish Bone

Man, verses mountain,
Feet against stone,
This adrenalin finds,
Equilibrium up there.

Descendants fountain,
A calling back home,
Love redialled,
Desire returns.

Haul in the summit,
Hoist the bone,
This Ritalin finds,
equality up there.

Decedent foundations,
Avalanche of stone,
Life dragged up a mountain,
To fall back home.

Yet who knows how the mountain got so high and
broken?

# Wish Bone

Man, verses mountain,
Feet against stone,
This adrenalin finds,
Equilibrium up there.

Descendants fountain,
A calling back home,
Love redialled,
Desire returns.

Haul in the summit,
Hoist the bone,
This Ritalin finds,
equality up there.

Decedent foundations,
Avalanche of stone,
Life dragged up a mountain,
To fall back home.

Yet who knows how the mountain got so high and
broken?

# One, Two, Three...

Rock, paper, scissor;
This poem wraps stone
Rock sharpens the scissor
The scissor cuts this poem
My love poem is shredded
Tangled in a bin like spaghetti
Discarded; never wedded
Words printed upon confetti
*Every, kiss, blown;*
Stolen with a gust
My words are empty
I'm all out of love.

## Full Stop (no more tears,,,,)

My internal dialogue intensity
Was released for you momentarily
Yet I fail to describe love in punctuation
Then I try to depict care in its absence
Where by a simple coma could accomplish
What my words alone could not
But all I have is this  .

# One, Two, Three...

Rock, paper, scissor;
This poem wraps stone
Rock sharpens the scissor
The scissor cuts this poem
My love poem is shredded
Tangled in a bin like spaghetti
Discarded; never wedded
Words printed upon confetti
*Every, kiss, blown;*
Stolen with a gust
My words are empty
I'm all out of love.

### Full Stop (no more tears,,,)

My internal dialogue intensity
Was released for you momentarily
Yet I fail to describe love in punctuation
Then I try to depict care in its absence
Where by a simple coma could accomplish
What my words alone could not
But all I have is this .

## Ink Well

Influenza used to hibernate
But now has nowhere to go
Except to humans
They are moist and warm
Even when they feel cold
This field once had grasses breezing
Now the wind ruffles the paper
Of planning applications granted
No mouse in the ink here
Or bats, vowels, crickets, toads
No eco system
Just a system of destruction
An unaffordable home
Tawney owl cannot nest there
Water can't penetrate that driveway
Look not for the beaver near that place
All rivers flow in the drains
Or in floods running across the streets
Is that in the ink?
Why not have bats live in a roof
Above the bin storage unit?
Why not have compost heap areas
Deep set with access to its beneath?
Why not leave the landscape undulated
Wildlife corridors beneath the road
Why is there not a large pond?
No Wild flowers or log piles found
Why remove a tree
That is itself an eco-system
Why is there no path through the fences
For hedgehogs, badgers, foxes?
If you want a disease to spread,
Destroy its home to build your own
Then it might live with you instead.

## Ink Well

Influenza used to hibernate
But now has nowhere to go
Except to humans
They are moist and warm
Even when they feel cold
This field once had grasses breezing
Now the wind ruffles the paper
Of planning applications granted
No mouse in the ink here
Or bats, vowels, crickets, toads
No eco system
Just a system of destruction
An unaffordable home
Tawney owl cannot nest there
Water can't penetrate that driveway
Look not for the beaver near that place
All rivers flow in the drains
Or in floods running across the streets
Is that in the ink?
Why not have bats live in a roof
Above the bin storage unit?
Why not have compost heap areas
Deep set with access to its beneath?
Why not leave the landscape undulated
Wildlife corridors beneath the road
Why is there not a large pond?
No Wild flowers or log piles found
Why remove a tree
That is itself an eco-system
Why is there no path through the fences
For hedgehogs, badgers, foxes?
If you want a disease to spread,
Destroy its home to build your own
Then it might live with you instead.

### Pearly Whites

It is so still here,
Sound, light, motion.
The bird song forgotten,
But that one note remains.
The river was rushing by,
So the sun set in waters of the canal.
One moment in memory...

Open the old wooden gates,
Lift up beyond perspective.
Focus on the movement,
Right to left, left to right.
As distance feeds new,
The wonder of each retinal scan.
A memory surround...

Shedding our fabric,
Losing tears, hair, sweat, clippings,
Buried now in life abundance,
Yet fragile as elephant,
Threatened as rhino and pangolin.
Your teeth and nails could also be trophies.

Would you rather display them with a smile and a wave;

or in a bloody cabinet?

## Pearly Whites

It is so still here,
Sound, light, motion.
The bird song forgotten,
But that one note remains.
The river was rushing by,
So the sun set in waters of the canal.
One moment in memory...


Open the old wooden gates,
Lift up beyond perspective.
Focus on the movement,
Right to left, left to right.
As distance feeds new,
The wonder of each retinal scan.
A memory surround...


Shedding our fabric,
Losing tears, hair, sweat, clippings,
Buried now in life abundance,
Yet fragile as elephant,
Threatened as rhino and pangolin.
Your teeth and nails could also be trophies.

Would you rather display them with a smile and a wave;
or in a bloody cabinet?

# The Scarecrow

I am a scarecrow
There is nothing to protect
And no crow to descry
No seed to steal
No crop to murder
I am seasick
There is no water.

These dunes rise and fall
As the hour glass is turned
An hour to teach
Another to learn
I wear a pirate hat
And sailors coat
There is no boat.

I did my job too well
I kept them all away
Each night I scare the sun
I am afraid of the dark
There is a seed in my pocket
The sickle moon is in the sky
If only I could cry...

# The Scarecrow

I am a scarecrow
There is nothing to protect
And no crow to descry
No seed to steal
No crop to murder
I am seasick
There is no water.

These dunes rise and fall
As the hour glass is turned
An hour to teach
Another to learn
I wear a pirate hat
And sailors coat
There is no boat.


I did my job too well
I kept them all away
Each night I scare the sun
I am afraid of the dark
There is a seed in my pocket
The sickle moon is in the sky
If only I could cry...

## A life in frozen fear

When seeing such troubles
Engulfing others
He grew to shrink.
Those operations
So commanding
He could not conduct himself.
So first he sat
Still he was
But weight still pressed down.
And so he lied
Feet up
Head down
To save his joints
His cartilage sighed.
Bought electronic machines
Strapped them to his muscles
So he could keep up his strength.
He was so inclined
To live his whole life
lying down
Never standing up.
So afraid of death and decay
He preserved his life
But never lived.
Until his dying day- he finally moved.

## A life in frozen fear

When seeing such troubles
Engulfing others
He grew to shrink.
Those operations
So commanding
He could not conduct himself.
So first he sat
Still he was
But weight still pressed down.
And so he lied
Feet up
Head down
To save his joints
His cartilage sighed.
Bought electronic machines
Strapped them to his muscles
So he could keep up his strength.
He was so inclined
To live his whole life
lying down
Never standing up.
So afraid of death and decay
He preserved his life
But never lived.
Until his dying day- he finally moved.

## Bed Stricken

A thunder clap
Is not for you to administer
A lightning strike
Is not for your eye lashes
No demand is yours to offer
In the covering of your sins.
Be free to walk your own path
The zenith climbs ten thousand stairs
Reaches every bottom rung
Stolen tears and stolen distance
The zenith breaths in and cries
"Azimuth dismount!"
Then dies...


## The Fold (Islandisation)

These sheets were washed,
Conditioned,
These sheets were of the fold.

These sheets were creased,
They were ironed,
Brought back into the fold.

Made the thread,
To stitch the hide,
Together within the fold.

This hide was stretched,
Dried out,
They stitched to join our fold,

The concrete washed in rain,
Every fenced off island,
Tearing at the seams of every fold.

# Bed Stricken

A thunder clap
Is not for you to administer
A lightning strike
Is not for your eye lashes
No demand is yours to offer
In the covering of your sins.
Be free to walk your own path
The zenith climbs ten thousand stairs
Reaches every bottom rung
Stolen tears and stolen distance
The zenith breaths in and cries
"Azimuth dismount!"
Then dies...

## The Fold (Islandisation)

These sheets were washed,
Conditioned,
These sheets were of the fold.

These sheets were creased,
They were ironed,
Brought back into the fold.

Made the thread,
To stitch the hide,
Together within the fold.

This hide was stretched,
Dried out,
They stitched to join our fold,

The concrete washed in rain,
Every fenced off island,
Tearing at the seams of every fold.

## Cast Out

Within the mould
At times angry or sad
If they tip then slap
Would you notice marks
your mould left?

Within its in possession
Your mould leaves depressions
Can you stand alone by yourself
if they take your family photographs
and cut you out of them

Perhaps that slap in the face
was not your choice at all
Maybe friendship is a thing
valued not left to spoil

We learn to cast together
A new mould to cast another
To leave the nurturing marks
Of a father and a mother

# Cast Out

Within the mould
At times angry or sad
If they tip then slap
Would you notice marks
your mould left?

Within its in possession
Your mould leaves depressions
Can you stand alone by yourself
if they take your family photographs
and cut you out of them

Perhaps that slap in the face
was not your choice at all
Maybe friendship is a thing
valued not left to spoil

We learn to cast together
A new mould to cast another
To leave the nurturing marks
Of a father and a mother

# Casting

I cast my mind back
You cast out a hook
I dilute the memory
With each look
Through the eyelet

Knit the memories together
Cast a needle instead

But that protest
Was forgotten by the Gudgeon
That found itself reeled to the waiting net
Held by the hand of a curmudgeon
Who did not appreciate the Gudgeon
Getting him wet

## A windy day

Only take offence when offence is intended.

"Give me back my fence
I leant it to you without hesitance,
Yet borrowed is not owned,
Put back, what you blow down!"

And even if offence was intended,
You don't have to be offended.

# Casting

I cast my mind back
You cast out a hook
I dilute the memory
With each look
Through the eyelet

Knit the memories together
Cast a needle instead

But that protest
Was forgotten by the Gudgeon
That found itself reeled to the waiting net
Held by the hand of a curmudgeon
Who did not appreciate the Gudgeon
Getting him wet


## A windy day

Only take offence when offence is intended.

"Give me back my fence
I leant it to you without hesitance,
Yet borrowed is not owned,
Put back, what you blow down!"

And even if offence was intended,
You don't have to be offended.

# Tooo

How much is too much?
Falling into a state of burdening
Where the impoverished care
For those in poverty
When tech drives your job
And drops off your clients
At an automated hotel
When too much is the goal
The one percent that own the world
Tax them at two thousand percent
then give them the tax breaks
for employing more people,
for paying a decent wage
for donating in the future
Maybe they would be asking
How much is too much; instead?

## Memory

I am in all that remains in my absence
A rainbow in autumnal leaf litter
Warmth found beneath the fallen snow
I measure the gap but never the measure
I hear every sound yet filter
Through tears you search the pictures I gather
Then count your rings of growth
When you reach what you see as ending
We join once more, the ring expanding.

# Tooo

How much is too much?
Falling into a state of burdening
Where the impoverished care
For those in poverty
When tech drives your job
And drops off your clients
At an automated hotel
When too much is the goal
The one percent that own the world
Tax them at two thousand percent
then give them the tax breaks
for employing more people,
for paying a decent wage
for donating in the future
Maybe they would be asking
How much is too much; instead?


## Memory

I am in all that remains in my absence
A rainbow in autumnal leaf litter
Warmth found beneath the fallen snow
I measure the gap but never the measure
I hear every sound yet filter
Through tears you search the pictures I gather
Then count your rings of growth
When you reach what you see as ending
We join once more, the ring expanding.

# vivid dream

You pulled back the curtain
Exiting the belly
Walked over and saw me
As I held my lover
You thought her as property
Stolen well
Retrieved well from you
Into the abode of skin and timber
To a bed of hide to hide
You found us there and attacked
I the only one left alive
But only for a short time
Staggering through the trees
Blood weeping
As below I can see mammoths
Walking in regimental lines
I wake
I die

## An Armed Shell

Thunder cracked that egg above my slumber
My pulse echoing drew that moth
That light through wing- hazel spotted linen
Repeated diminishing pacing south
Karl Jenkins now does the same to me
Who else had ruined their own regret but me
I had spun on my heels completely
I only fired one shot, one shot was all I needed

It was the bullet that found me
So the mortar shell could not

# vivid dream

You pulled back the curtain
Exiting the belly
Walked over and saw me
As I held my lover
You thought her as property
Stolen well
Retrieved well from you
Into the abode of skin and timber
To a bed of hide to hide
You found us there and attacked
I the only one left alive
But only for a short time
Staggering through the trees
Blood weeping
As below I can see mammoths
Walking in regimental lines
I wake
I die

**An Armed Shell**

Thunder cracked that egg above my slumber
My pulse echoing drew that moth
That light through wing- hazel spotted linen
Repeated diminishing pacing south
Karl Jenkins now does the same to me
Who else had ruined their own regret but me
I had spun on my heels completely
I only fired one shot, one shot was all I needed

It was the bullet that found me
So the mortar shell could not

## Recycling

Cannot love in current
For rocks displaced
So to the source
Back to the lake
In that mirror glass
Please remember
My forgotten face
So I might forget
This mess I've made
There is refluence in me
A pulling of a thread
Until all this knit
Has been saved
I'm all out of yarn
A basket case


## Any End

The snow starts falling
You buy some cards
Wishing for good will to all
Let's have a jolly time
That snow keeps falling
You sign your name
Upon each card
Others do the same
You gather them together
Don your warmest wools
Then out, out into the storm
The snow has blocked up every door
Back home then, to lonely and warm

## Recycling

Cannot love in current
For rocks displaced
So to the source
Back to the lake
In that mirror glass
Please remember
My forgotten face
So I might forget
This mess I've made
There is refluence in me
A pulling of a thread
Until all this knit
Has been saved
I'm all out of yarn
A basket case


## Any End

The snow starts falling
You buy some cards
Wishing for good will to all
Let's have a jolly time
That snow keeps falling
You sign your name
Upon each card
Others do the same
You gather them together
Don your warmest wools
Then out, out into the storm
The snow has blocked up every door
Back home then, to lonely and warm

# A squirrel

Movement seen,
A feather, a leaf,
No not a leaf,
Maybe shadows of leaves.
This curiosity,
Keeps my gaze as
Grass does a cow,
Chewing still when
Looking up, and now
Looking down, I could
That movement see
In my inner mindfulness
Swallowing my curiosity.
A tail satisfies
Then intrigue ensues,
A fly fisherman casting
Catches my curiosity anew.
Then curious eyes
Poke out from the side
Our curious meeting
Of curious minds.

# A squirrel

Movement seen,
A feather, a leaf,
No not a leaf,
Maybe shadows of leaves.
This curiosity,
Keeps my gaze as
Grass does a cow,
Chewing still when
Looking up, and now
Looking down, I could
That movement see
In my inner mindfulness
Swallowing my curiosity.
A tail satisfies
Then intrigue ensues,
A fly fisherman casting
Catches my curiosity anew.
Then curious eyes
Poke out from the side
Our curious meeting
Of curious minds.

## Marbles I've Lost

I was late to wake
To marble your mind   ?
You got the last bus
I got the next one mind
I was late to never
Cut into that line
That dream ended
I woke up then died

Found my shovel
Started to dig my own grave
Another job half done
I was born again
Into the midst of mid life
But left there that crisis ends
I rig a sundial to ring a bell
I will not be late again

I was right on time today
This jet is a spiralling stair
Seen within each marble
I wave to you from the chair
Of this stair lift rising
Wrinkled my skin, grey my hair
If I fall again, my grave half dug
If you die first; could we please share?

## Marbles I've Lost

I was late to wake
To marble your mind   ?
You got the last bus
I got the next one mind
I was late to never
Cut into that line
That dream ended
I woke up then died

Found my shovel
Started to dig my own grave
Another job half done
I was born again
Into the midst of mid life
But left there that crisis ends
I rig a sundial to ring a bell
I will not be late again

I was right on time today
This jet is a spiralling stair
Seen within each marble
I wave to you from the chair
Of this stair lift rising
Wrinkled my skin, grey my hair
If I fall again, my grave half dug
If you die first; could we please share?

**Anode**

DC shakes its head
AC spins it around
Cathode array thinks a while
Then has a long sit down
Magnetic deflected
Defeats the objective
So made the green screen frown
Regress in theory viewed
Digress in theory spied
Back to the drawing board
With the lot of you
Science is neither proof
Or of that proof denied


**Silent Rain**

And now this dust
This blue sky and dust
This rainforest brought rain
Once
Now dust

This rain stick
An extension from each hand
Held only the sound
A tear
Upon dust

Take what is left of the trees
Hollow them out
Carve your names into each rock
Put that dust into each stick

And dance in silent dust.

**Anode**

DC shakes its head
AC spins it around
Cathode array thinks a while
Then has a long sit down
Magnetic deflected
Defeats the objective
So made the green screen frown
Regress in theory viewed
Digress in theory spied
Back to the drawing board
With the lot of you
Science is neither proof
Or of that proof denied


**Silent Rain**

And now this dust
This blue sky and dust
This rainforest brought rain
Once
Now dust

This rain stick
An extension from each hand
Held only the sound
A tear
Upon dust

Take what is left of the trees
Hollow them out
Carve your names into each rock
Put that dust into each stick

And dance in silent dust.

# No Margin for Error

And yet I had no morning
A4 paper is lined with horizons
I can write deep into the ocean
You can dip your toe; into the ink
But my soul you say is setting
This path an upward climb
I cannot grip to a meaning
Or ascertain the time

You gave me this four-leaf clover
You sent to me this land mine
I need to be careful with each step
Even a gifted seed is not mine
So, as I delve down along this seam
Of each Canary that ceased to sing
A tunnel dug with no destination
But death; that is a guarantee

I had no margin for error
An alarm bell was distant ringing
Flame of candles consumed in dark
Dust to dust; coughing echoing
Suffocating, weightlessness and weary
This cage seeming quite contrary
What strength wove these lines
Upon which I write whilst dyeing

# No Margin for Error

And yet I had no morning
A4 paper is lined with horizons
I can write deep into the ocean
You can dip your toe; into the ink
But my soul you say is setting
This path an upward climb
I cannot grip to a meaning
Or ascertain the time

You gave me this four-leaf clover
You sent to me this land mine
I need to be careful with each step
Even a gifted seed is not mine
So, as I delve down along this seam
Of each Canary that ceased to sing
A tunnel dug with no destination
But death; that is a guarantee

I had no margin for error
An alarm bell was distant ringing
Flame of candles consumed in dark
Dust to dust; coughing echoing
Suffocating, weightlessness and weary
This cage seeming quite contrary
What strength wove these lines
Upon which I write whilst dyeing

# {Butterflies in a frame}

### act1
### (The dealer criticises the collector)
Each time you bat an eyelid
You reveal your true intent
Don't go searching with that ring
Kneeling to those you've not yet met
Love may settle down beside you
If you stop waving around that net
Mars wealds no weapon seeking love
And Venus has no trap set

### act2
### (The collector awaits in stillness)
When at last you find your mate
And together you rest near me
So those silent thoughts capillaries
Set pulse to beat each wing
If I could decipher such an exchange
What words could fill space between?
"Have patience lepidopterist
Love is such a fragile thing"

### act3
### (The collector realises his own undoing)
And so I had finally trapped you
Such a pure love needed to be saved
I peered beneath the glass in wonder
Then attached a blank price tag to the frame
But it fluttered causing me to jump
I groped desperately for the priceless in vain
The pane of glass shattered upon impact
The butterflies flew away

# {Butterflies in a frame}

## act1
### (The dealer criticises the collector)
Each time you bat an eyelid
You reveal your true intent
Don't go searching with that ring
Kneeling to those you've not yet met
Love may settle down beside you
If you stop waving around that net
Mars wealds no weapon seeking love
And Venus has no trap set

## act2
### (The collector awaits in stillness)
When at last you find your mate
And together you rest near me
So those silent thoughts capillaries
Set pulse to beat each wing
If I could decipher such an exchange
What words could fill space between?
"Have patience lepidopterist
Love is such a fragile thing"

## act3
### (The collector realises his own undoing)
And so I had finally trapped you
Such a pure love needed to be saved
I peered beneath the glass in wonder
Then attached a blank price tag to the frame
But it fluttered causing me to jump
I groped desperately for the priceless in vain
The pane of glass shattered upon impact
The butterflies flew away

# The Table Cloth

With so much arrayed
A feast to behold
Crystal that blinks
Earthenware that warms
Candles lit there
Cutlery precise
Perhaps then you grab me
By the scruff of my neck
And pull so hard and fast
Removing me from the table
To such applause and delight
Whipped from your table
Disturbing nothing else
Your sleeve holds five aces
Three are of diamond
One of both club and spade
Yet no heart

# The Table Cloth

With so much arrayed
A feast to behold
Crystal that blinks
Earthenware that warms
Candles lit there
Cutlery precise
Perhaps then you grab me
By the scruff of my neck
And pull so hard and fast
Removing me from the table
To such applause and delight
Whipped from your table
Disturbing nothing else
Your sleeve holds five aces
Three are of diamond
One of both club and spade
Yet no heart

# Check Mate

The house of cards collapsed
They arranged themselves in ranks
The King of Diamonds led his army
To shuffle themselves into a pack

The King of Clubs sent a scouting party
To spy out the best route
The movements of the Diamonds were known
And so, they followed suit

The King of Spades ordered a trench be dug
Arranged his army in a defensive position
The King of Hearts saw this as an act of war
Arranged his army in opposition

Sent forth from the Club encampment
To bolster the strength of Spades
A Rook a Knight and Bishop
Ten, Seven and Jack their names

From the Hearts was sent an envoy
To seek assistance from the Diamond King
A Rook a Knight and a Bishop were sold to Hearts
As Diamonds valued fairness above all things

And so thus they were aligned
With sixteen pieces each
Rules of engagement were devised
And a time limit was also agreed

# Check Mate

The house of cards collapsed
They arranged themselves in ranks
The King of Diamonds led his army
To shuffle themselves into a pack

The King of Clubs sent a scouting party
To spy out the best route
The movements of the Diamonds were known
And so, they followed suit

The King of Spades ordered a trench be dug
Arranged his army in a defensive position
The King of Hearts saw this as an act of war
Arranged his army in opposition

Sent forth from the Club encampment
To bolster the strength of Spades
A Rook a Knight and Bishop
Ten, Seven and Jack their names

From the Hearts was sent an envoy
To seek assistance from the Diamond King
A Rook a Knight and a Bishop were sold to Hearts
As Diamonds valued fairness above all things

And so thus they were aligned
With sixteen pieces each
Rules of engagement were devised
And a time limit was also agreed

The Ace of Hearts made the first move
And took two steps before the King
That set the tempo to such a war
Then quickly both Queens were killed

Being but a Pawn
The Ace of hearts fought on
The Knights were slain, the Rooks to rubble
Each Bishops prayer heeded by none

And so, the Ace yet a simple Pawn
Lifted the fallen Queens crown to her own head
Checking the King of Spades last ditch attempts
They saw that all others were dead

The King and his crowned Ace of Hearts
Stood alone triumphant and so went to bed
Twist, snap, stick, they folded together
An Ace so high would soon be wed

But morning brought a reshuffle
And a new house of cards was built
Each and every card had been retrieved
From wherever they had been spilt

The King and Ace of Hearts
Were found lying crumpled together
Beside them was a brand-new card
The dealer named it The Joker

The Ace of Hearts made the first move
And took two steps before the King
That set the tempo to such a war
Then quickly both Queens were killed

Being but a Pawn
The Ace of hearts fought on
The Knights were slain, the Rooks to rubble
Each Bishops prayer heeded by none

And so, the Ace yet a simple Pawn
Lifted the fallen Queens crown to her own head
Checking the King of Spades last ditch attempts
They saw that all others were dead

The King and his crowned Ace of Hearts
Stood alone triumphant and so went to bed
Twist, snap, stick, they folded together
An Ace so high would soon be wed

But morning brought a reshuffle
And a new house of cards was built
Each and every card had been retrieved
From wherever they had been spilt

The King and Ace of Hearts
Were found lying crumpled together
Beside them was a brand-new card
The dealer named it The Joker

## THE PRESUMPTUOUS MAN-
## TALKS TO THE INVISABLE MAN

I am sorry to have kept you waiting
Can I take your coat?
No?
There is no need to be shy,
You will find I have seen it all,
and I understand.

Your predicament is troubling you,
But a problem shared is a problem halved/
and none are indivisible.
One lump or two?
No?
Please do take a seat.

I have looked over your file,
It says you struggle to be noticed.
I am here.
I am aware of you,
and I care!
So please acknowledge me!!

Perhaps we could start again.
I am sorry to have kept you waiting,
But I have been avoiding you.
If I dare look in to the mirror,
Will I like what I see?
Will I see you?
Or will you see me?

## THE PRESUMPTUOUS MAN-
## TALKS TO THE INVISABLE MAN

I am sorry to have kept you waiting
Can I take your coat?
No?
There is no need to be shy,
You will find I have seen it all,
and I understand.

Your predicament is troubling you,
But a problem shared is a problem halved/
and none are indivisible.
One lump or two?
No?
Please do take a seat.

I have looked over your file,
It says you struggle to be noticed.
I am here.
I am aware of you,
and I care!
So please acknowledge me!!

Perhaps we could start again.
I am sorry to have kept you waiting,
But I have been avoiding you.
If I dare look in to the mirror,
Will I like what I see?
Will I see you?
Or will you see me?

# The Field

Every element is of smaller elements
God is the infinite
Every element within the same field flowing
God flows within each

Every star is also an element
God has a grand design
The field created all matter
God is the infinite creator

Time fills the hour glass with sand

To every seed
The field
To every death
The field

Up from down
Aspire from diminish
Love from longing
God is the infinite divider

To each angelic personality
God is gifting to all creatures
Gifting to you sleep
As a breeze moves though a field

God is gifting to you such dreams

Your raiment is kept safe within every memory
None are forgotten
God is forgiving

Look into the mirror you see yourself
Yet God flows within you and within everything else

# The Field

Every element is of smaller elements
God is the infinite
Every element within the same field flowing
God flows within each

Every star is also an element
God has a grand design
The field created all matter
God is the infinite creator

Time fills the hour glass with sand

To every seed
The field
To every death
The field

Up from down
Aspire from diminish
Love from longing
God is the infinite divider

To each angelic personality
God is gifting to all creatures
Gifting to you sleep
As a breeze moves though a field

God is gifting to you such dreams

Your raiment is kept safe within every memory
None are forgotten
God is forgiving

Look into the mirror you see yourself
Yet God flows within you and within everything else

## Spinning Jenny

What seeds these cotton clouds
Drawn across the sun
Grey they seem on days so bleak
The silver not yet spun
It seems a yarn pulls at the seams
As each seam comes undone
Down will pour the pannus threading
Forecast but yet to come

Below the basalt sky foreboding
That pushes this over grown sea
I'll follow this inversion deep
Yet be way led to pastures green
What has become of this cataract sky
And of this path once clear to me
No stars to get my bearings or heart
I walk so lost yet free

To tread the path of unmade moss
To sink slightly with each step
If cotton pulled to bake the peat
A crunch with each footfall yet
Wind ever on a lonely path
Perhaps a happiness there
For threads become intertwined
And on these paths we'll meet again

## Spinning Jenny

What seeds these cotton clouds
Drawn across the sun
Grey they seem on days so bleak
The silver not yet spun
It seems a yarn pulls at the seams
As each seam comes undone
Down will pour the pannus threading
Forecast but yet to come

Below the basalt sky foreboding
That pushes this over grown sea
I'll follow this inversion deep
Yet be way led to pastures green
What has become of this cataract sky
And of this path once clear to me
No stars to get my bearings or heart
I walk so lost yet free

To tread the path of unmade moss
To sink slightly with each step
If cotton pulled to bake the peat
A crunch with each footfall yet
Wind ever on a lonely path
Perhaps a happiness there
For threads become intertwined
And on these paths we'll meet again

## Flint Stone Circle Drum

And in the foreground stones raised upright before me

How were these stones brought here?
What were they placed here for?
If I was given such a task
How could I have done it; and what for?

First the stone is wrapped
The stone is drilled
The hole filled with water, then capped
A cold winter gives an honest break

The stone set in timber roll
So as to roll, when hauled

Then I think of you
And align each placement of stone with the stars

To what purpose I then propose
As my heart beats for you my love
To strike each stone that is present
And hear the note most prevalent

Wrapping the stones in furs
To make a space that is warm inside

Stretching tightly, a roof skin over the stones

So you can hear the drum beating with every rain drop...

# Flint Stone Circle Drum

And in the foreground stones raised upright before me

How were these stones brought here?
What were they placed here for?
If I was given such a task
How could I have done it; and what for?

First the stone is wrapped
The stone is drilled
The hole filled with water, then capped
A cold winter gives an honest break

The stone set in timber roll
So as to roll, when hauled

Then I think of you
And align each placement of stone with the stars

To what purpose I then propose
As my heart beats for you my love
To strike each stone that is present
And hear the note most prevalent

Wrapping the stones in furs
To make a space that is warm inside

Stretching tightly, a roof skin over the stones

So you can hear the drum beating with every rain drop...

## Feedback

My guitar knows not my pain
The strings' tension
Cutting deep into the bridges
And as my fingers delay
Each muted note falls away.
I will spend some time with sorrow
Cradling you with love
Do not think of yourself as cheap
I have also been self-judged
Crazy, lazy, alcoholic;
I just need tuning
Like you
Every now and then

## In Your Opinion

An opinion should be scratched in sand
not carved in granite.
And as you scratch, should a pin drop
and ring out; you should listen to it.
Balance what you once saw on one side
And what you see now on the other.
Then hold out your argument, as you would
a heavy mirror.

## Feedback

My guitar knows not my pain
The strings' tension
Cutting deep into the bridges
And as my fingers delay
Each muted note falls away.
I will spend some time with sorrow
Cradling you with love
Do not think of yourself as cheap
I have also been self-judged
Crazy, lazy, alcoholic;
I just need tuning
Like you
Every now and then

## In Your Opinion

An opinion should be scratched in sand
not carved in granite.
And as you scratch, should a pin drop
and ring out; you should listen to it.
Balance what you once saw on one side
And what you see now on the other.
Then hold out your argument, as you would
a heavy mirror.

# Reunions

I feel like I've walked on this road before
Each time I turn around to see from where I've come
Since we parted all has been barren
And where our path first met is hidden
Yet here at the pinnacle, a view of things to come
And a beautiful landscape stretches towards the horizon

A path running parallel to mine joins up ahead
Should I race to catch you or wait for you instead?
I hear your voice calling to me on the breeze
The rush of memory the twang of my heart string
I call out your name, I wait as I stand
Soon we will walk together hand in hand

## Exit Stage Right

Enamoured to descry in fortitude
Such a descent and crisis met
Vertigo sets to work itself in latitudes
The inner ear spins about the precipice
What cowardly act you say then followed?
A trapeze dancing on a high wire
Crawling to the brink yet then falter
Gripping tight with such fear so dire

So brave to try to deny such fate
As had been fated to befall
Grief fell to its death that day
Guilt in its stead was born
To every cloud a silhouette of silver
Of tears forbade yet to fall
Don't look for fault or go seeking blame
The alarm rang, my time here was done

## Reunions

I feel like I've walked on this road before
Each time I turn around to see from where I've come
Since we parted all has been barren
And where our path first met is hidden
Yet here at the pinnacle, a view of things to come
And a beautiful landscape stretches towards the horizon

A path running parallel to mine joins up ahead
Should I race to catch you or wait for you instead?
I hear your voice calling to me on the breeze
The rush of memory the twang of my heart string
I call out your name, I wait as I stand
Soon we will walk together hand in hand


## Exit Stage Right

Enamoured to descry in fortitude
Such a descent and crisis met
Vertigo sets to work itself in latitudes
The inner ear spins about the precipice
What cowardly act you say then followed?
A trapeze dancing on a high wire
Crawling to the brink yet then falter
Gripping tight with such fear so dire

So brave to try to deny such fate
As had been fated to befall
Grief fell to its death that day
Guilt in its stead was born
To every cloud a silhouette of silver
Of tears forbade yet to fall
Don't look for fault or go seeking blame
The alarm rang, my time here was done

# Head-In-Rain

Casing out line after line
Then catching his own reflection
Only rain could provide shelter
From the storm he was lost in
Forgetting then his own purpose
Mountain peaks bite the distance
Cutting the sky as he turned
To see the sun setting in blood.
A king fisher then landed
Upon the fisherman's rod
Then cast itself
For need not want
Then his focus that had been drawn
On distant mountains
And on the water's surface,
Turned on him suddenly
And so, he waded tirelessly
Attempting to escape
But fate can be very creative
Trapping the unsuspecting in a dream
An old wooden gate in reflection
And beneath it; this refluent stream.

# Head-In-Rain

Casing out line after line
Then catching his own reflection
Only rain could provide shelter
From the storm he was lost in
Forgetting then his own purpose
Mountain peaks bite the distance
Cutting the sky as he turned
To see the sun setting in blood.
A king fisher then landed
Upon the fisherman's rod
Then cast itself
For need not want
Then his focus that had been drawn
On distant mountains
And on the water's surface,
Turned on him suddenly
And so, he waded tirelessly
Attempting to escape
But fate can be very creative
Trapping the unsuspecting in a dream
An old wooden gate in reflection
And beneath it; this refluent stream.

# INDEX OF FIRST LINES

26; The shadow saw a light
26; Birds of a feather,
27; Deep down into this old chair
27; I sit in an old chair
28; We evaporated together
29; And
30; I rode that wave
30; To describe each leaf as it falls,
31; Forgive if you can my falling as rain,
31; I don't like to leave
32; I broke the fulcrum,
33; From a love spawned,
34; Plectrum web woven,
34; To dance is the heaven
35; Pondering where I am,
35; Proud is to strict,
36; Join the individual's group,
36; What's on your mind?
37; Ode to fly
37; Fat Track
38; You could replace that broken door
38; Up shoots the thread
39; A description
39; When love is but a torn sail,
40; A fisherman prepared his line, an anchor
41; We are equal you and I,
41; First carried
42; Of love and loss
42; The sky tonight
43; Shaped by shadows,
43; I'm losing my hair
44; How slow this sorrow
45; These same shadows moved faster than he
45; The sun dial struck ten

46; Immediate so soon,
46; But a thimble
47; With quill poised
47; When I was born into this life
48; For some to bridge
49; Psychological amplitude tested,
49; To sleep...
50; I thought I'd have said by now
50; No holds- bard,
51; I thought it a dam,
51; I thought to walk
52; The longest day lasted, for what you'd call ten,
52; Until the killick
53; Some give each step tile and texture
53; I'd been struck by cupid's arrow
54; This world- round once,
54; The picture in which I live
55; Bannister of all affection
55; Tuning forks A, C and D,
56; I did not fall
56; I had a glass full whisky
57; There was always a mountain to climb
57; The humble chart
58; What will you inherit?
58; Should you choose next time
59; My birth a string plucked
59; And we greet them as dear friends
60; But not a day has any day
60; Over the top for some
61; The soldier engulfed in a common confusion,
61; Rose gripped tight
61; Buttons for bullets,
62; Perhaps they found an alpine butterfly,
62; You hold on tight
63; I am a danger

64; The image from a magazine,
64; Determined to turn over a new leaf
65; Within a rainbow,
65; When a table has a missing leg
66; As if time itself had lost all sense of direction
66; Too bold casting shadows
67; That moment when I arrive
67; If you want to write, but have no pen,
68; Cast the line out
68; At the centre of a droid,
69; Another step,
70; Time spent well,
70; My thought origin,
71; I was wondering about what it is to wonder,
72; A beat to work to; helps
73; Man, verses mountain,
74; Rock, paper, scissor;
74; My internal dialogue intensity
75; Influenza used to hibernate
76; It is so still here,
77; I am a scarecrow
78; When seeing such troubles
79; A thunder clap
79; These sheets were washed,
80; Within the mould
81; I cast my mind back
81; Only take offence when offence is intended.
82; How much is too much?
82; I am in all that remains in my absence
83; You pulled back the curtain
83; Thunder cracked that egg above my slumber
84; Cannot love in current
84; The snow starts falling
85; Movement seen,
86; I was late to wake

87; DC shakes its head
87; And now this dust
88; And yet I had no morning
89; Each time you bat an eyelid
90; With so much arrayed
91; The house of cards collapsed
93; I am sorry to have kept you waiting
94; Every element is of smaller elements
95; What seeds these cotton clouds
96; And in the foreground stones raised upright before me
97; My guitar knows not my pain
97; An opinion should be scratched in sand
98; I feel like I've walked on this road before
98; Enamoured to descry in fortitude
99; Casing out line after line

# Index of Verses

**41;** Equilibrium
**48;** Etc.
**58;** Each Rung
**98;** Exit Stage Right

 **5;** Fossilised Remanences
**17;** Feel the Strain
**37;** Fat Track
**67;** FOLDED PAPER BOAT
**96;** Flint Stone Circle Drum
**74;** Full Stop (no more tears,,,)
**61;** Forget Me Not
**62;** Forget me knot
**97;** Feedback
**69;** For Love

**17;** Hour hand
 **3;** Homesick
**57; dew**
**99;** Head-In-Rain

**13;** I Made My Bed
**42;** Incomplete
**75;** Ink Well
**97;** In Your Opinion

**23;** Joints
**53;** Journeymen
**53;** Jupiter

**51;** Listed memory
**25;** Life Addiction
**56;** Liquid Lens O

**82;** Memory
**36;** Mindful Restoration
**86;** Marbles I've Lost

**19;** Nail Clippings
**60;** Not A Day
**38;** Nothing Rhymes with Orange
**88;** No Margin for Error

# Glossary of Terms

*Authors note;*
*We each learn language in our own way. Very often it is from hearing others use words within context with other words in a sentence, that we assume meaning. Rather than by studying dictionaries to learn the words wider accepted meaning. There by, we all have our own unique language; since a meaning of a word to you might be different to the meaning of that same word to another person. So, the Glossary is intended not as a Dictionary, but as a guide due to my neglecting to consult one.*

**and;** Logic gate where by all inputs only- give an output.

**autumnal;** Of the season when leaves typically change colour then fall.

**anode;** Positive terminal.

**apogee;** A world away- the dark side of the moon- communication not possible.

**bridge;** String musical instrument vibration retainer/ a means to overcome an obstacle.

**binary;** 0 and 1, on and off, Morse code etc. Data communication method.

**bow;** The forward most part of a boats hull.

**bobbin;** A cylinder that stores thread that is wound around it.

**bannister;** A walking aid that helps prevent trips and falls.

**bumblebeeing;** Motion in response to external influences.

**capo;** A movable string musical instrument vibration retainer.

**clipping;** To reduce or limit (eg. voltage, current, length, time etc.).

**cataract;** That which was once clear yet no longer is so.

**cathode;** Negative terminal.

**cumulous;** A fair weather fluffy cloud.

**curmudgeon;** A very grumpy person.

**cathode array;** Resulting image on an oscilloscope or old TV screen.

**candela;** A candle with burning wick.

**Cheshire cat;** A cat with orange fur.

**dominium;** Responsibility inherent to care for that which is under your control.

**dissident;** A challenging debate where by both sides disagree.

**dolorous;** A peaceful inner joy.

**diablo;** Egg timer shaped object flung in the air then caught again on a taught string.

**dunnock;** A species of sparrow.

**diluted;** To add water.

**extrapolate;** To continue to add (eg. distance, detail).

**equinox;** Relating to the orbit of the moon and earth- half way between both summer and winter solstices.

**eyelet;** The hole in a needle through which a thread is secured.
**eg;** For example.
**etc;** And so on.

**fold;** A grouping due to one single action (eg. chess pieces moving to the centre as the board folds inwards on a board that folds (a normal one} ).
**fulcrum;** The point at which a mechanical scale pivots/ the balancing point.
**furrow;** The undulations of land due to ploughing or of skin wrinkles due to frowning or smiling.

**Gudgeon;** A species of fish.

**hyoscine;** A truth serum/ travel sickness drug.
**hexadecimal;** Number system with the base of 16.

**inversion;** To climb as high as you can/ the water surface that fish can't swim beyond/ a nimbus spreading out as the water elements reach their upper limits of rising into the sky.
**Islandisation;** Creation of places of isolation.
**impasse;** Where one path divides into more paths- and the choice of the next path is undecided.

**jettison;** Abandon or discard intentionally
**Jackson Pollok;** He was an artist.

**keel;** The spine of a ship.
**kaleidoscopic;** The colours of the iris / the view through a kaleidoscope.
**killick;** A stone anchor for a small boat.
**knit;** Interwoven woollen fabric/ separate fabrics woven together.

**lapilli;** Small volcanic rocks.
**logic gate;** An electronic switch.
**lawn;** Tended grass in the yard.
**Lye;** A salty solution.
**labyrinthine;** To be lost.
**Lenticularis;** An oval shaped cloud that can look like a UFO.
**lepidopterologist;** Someone who studies butterflies.

**nautical mile;** To underestimate (eg. effort, distance travelled) / swimming against the tide remaining stationary to the shore line / to climb a mountain or wave adding effort not distance.
**nor;** Logic gate where by no input gives an output.
**nadir;** The skies above the south pole.
**neap;** Seasonally calm tide.
**nimbus;** A cloud that attempts to push beyond its inversion.

**or;** Logic gate where by either one or both inputs only- give an output

**opus;** Work/ to create music.

**obsidian;** A light volcanic glass.

**pannus;** Rainfall seem from a distance as a hazy shadow beneath a distant cloud.

**plectrum;** Implement used to pluck the strings of musical instruments.

**Polaris;** The star that is positioned above the North Pole that is often used to aid navigation.

**paling;** To become pale or diluted/ obscured by mist or fog.

**pearly whites;** teeth.

**refluent;** Water moving against the main body of water/ to rebel/ to regress.

**refluence;** To move in the opposite direction to the surrounding flow direction.

**root, mean, square;** Three different ways to calculate the same thing (the average) with different results. Calculating a course or position on a nautical map made complex by variables.

**Ritalin;** A highly addictive drug used to treat attention deficit hyperactivity disorder

**remanences;** Field memory- to remain whilst seeming absent.

**reminiscence;** Distant memory- spontaneous recollection.

**regress;** To want to relive a past experience/ to revert to a previous state.

**stern;** Rear of a ship or boat/ to control by imposing will.

**sill;** Exterior ledge of a window frame.

**silhouette;** Shape of object made of neither the object nor the background, but of shadow or diffused light.

**siphon;** A continuous transfer of energy or state e.g. combustion/fluid transfer.

**Sunday best;** To dress up smartly to attend church.

**sod;** A tuft of grass.

**scarecrow;** A seed protector.

**spinning jenny;** A wooden machine used to make thread.

**tiller;** Used to steer a boat.

**tinker;** A mischievous child/ a childish drunken adult.

**uniform;** As to look the same.

**verb;** A doing word.

**venal;** Being dishonest.

**wick;** That which is protruding from a fuel source anticipating flame.

**x axis;** Horizontal divisible line of a graph.

**yarn;** Fleece that is spun to a long cord on a spinning jenny or a story extrapolated.

**y axis;** Vertical divisible line of a graph.

**zenith;** The skies above the north pole.

# Notes.

# Notes.

# Notes.

Ingram Content Group UK Ltd.
Milton Keynes UK
UKHW041054300323
419409UK00014B/503/J